SCANDALS!

Rogues, Rascals and Infamy
in
Hull and East Yorkshire

Angus Young

Highgate of Beverley

Highgate Publications (Beverley) Limited
2011

British Library Cataloguing in Publication Data.
A catalogue record for this book is available from the British Library.

ISBN 978 1902645 575

Published by
Highgate of Beverley

Highgate Publications (Beverley) Limited
24 Wylies Road, Beverley, HU17 7AP
Telephone (01482) 866826

Produced by
Highgate Print Limited
24 Wylies Road, Beverley, HU17 7AP
Telephone (01482) 866826

Contents

Photo Credits

Hull Daily Mail, Hull City Council, Shona Singleton and Christopher S. Sykes.

Acknowledgements

My love and thanks to Alison for her enduring patience and support since I first got the idea for this book a mere 12 years ago !

Introduction

WHAT IS SCANDAL and why does it have a seemingly endless power to fascinate us?

I kept asking myself these two recurring questions during the research and writing of this book.

Perhaps William Shakespeare hit the nail on the head in his poem *The Rape of Lucrece* when he wrote: 'The mightier man, the mightier is the thing/That makes him honoured or begets him hate;/For greatest scandal waits on greatest state.' As in Shakespeare's time, those in power still tend to generate today's biggest scandals, perhaps because they are seen as having most to lose and furthest to fall.

This collection of some of the best-known rogues, rascals and scandalous bad behaviour seen in Hull and East Yorkshire over the last 150 years or so is by no means a definitive history.

Some stories, such as the £45,000 football transfer bung allegedly collected from a fish box unloaded from an Icelandic trawler at Hull docks on behalf of the late Nottingham Forest manager Brian Clough, will have to wait for another day before being given the full justice they probably deserve. Others, such as the almost entirely man-made disaster that was the June 2007 floods and the accompanying attempts by some to falsely pin all the blame on Mother Nature, probably warrant a book all of their own. As for John Prescott's affair with his diary secretary while he was still serving as the country's Deputy Prime Minister, perhaps enough has already been written.

Most of the scandals featured here very much reflect the age in which they occurred. Members of the Royal family no longer spend their weekends playing illegal card games in the homes of local wealthy tycoons, while bribery and corruption is hopefully a thing of the past in the corridors of power at our local councils. However, some of the darker episodes in the lives of well-known figures of their day such as Amy

Johnson and David Whitfield do have parallels with today's celebrity-fixated culture where scandals have almost become the norm.

Chapter 1

A Royal Scandal

SITTING NEXT TO HER LAWYER, the woman dressed in a dark jacket, maroon plaid skirt and white blouse was described on the court list as Laurence, Anne Elizabeth Alice Louise, date of birth 15/08/50. However, this was no ordinary defendant appearing before the bench at Slough magistrates' court in November 2002. The Princess Royal – better known as Princess Anne – was there to plead guilty to being in charge of a dog, namely a three-year-old English bull terrier bitch called Dotty, which had caused injury in a public place.

Accompanied by her husband and two children, the Princess spoke only twice during the hour-long hearing, replying 'It is,' when asked to confirm her name and 'Yup' to confirm her address. Otherwise, it was left to others to describe how Dotty attacked two young boys while being taken for a walk in Great Windsor Park. The eldest, a 12-year-old, had suffered a small bite to his collarbone, while his seven-year-old cousin escaped with scratches to his forearm, back and leg.

Addressing the court, defence barrister Hugo Keith found himself in the rare position of offering mitigating circumstances on behalf of the daughter of a reigning monarch.

'By her plea of guilty, the Princess Royal has acknowledged responsibility for the actions of Dotty,' he said. 'It is quite clear that her first action after putting Dotty in the back of the car was to apologise profusely for what had happened.' Mr Keith went on to tell the court how the Princess and her husband had offered assistance in getting medical help for the boys in the wake of the incident and, as responsible dog owners, had willingly provided their details to the police. 'Dotty, like many of her breed, is a good-natured dog, wholly lacking in malice,' he added.

Several months after the case Dotty undermined his argument when she attacked and killed one of the Queen's beloved corgis. By then, however, the Princess Royal had already earned herself a place in the comparatively short but colourful history of court appearances by members of the Royal family. Fined £500 and ordered to pay £250 compensation to each of the boys attacked by Dotty, the magistrates allowed her seven days to pay – a more palatable punishment than the penalty of death by beheading handed out by a court to King Charles I some three and a half centuries earlier.

Until Dotty's intervention, Charles' trial was the last time a Royal had been arraigned in an English court but it certainly wasn't the most recent courtroom appearance by a member of the Royal family. That dubious honour belonged to the then Prince of Wales, later to become Edward VII, who was called to give evidence in a case which became known as one of East Yorkshire's most infamous scandals. Referred to as either the Tranby Croft Affair or the Baccarat Scandal, the case caused a sensation in 1890s London society largely because it contained all the ingredients of a classic pot-boiler – the aristocracy, illicit gambling and what eventually became a very public accusation of cheating.

It revolved around a visit by the Prince of Wales and a party of friends to the Anlaby home of wealthy Hull shipping tycoon Arthur Wilson during St Leger week, the highlight of the horse-racing calendar at Doncaster racecourse. At the time, the family-owned Wilson Line was one of the biggest shipping companies in the world and both Wilson's Tranby Croft home and the social circles he moved in reflected his status as one of the most influential industrialists of his day.

Entertaining the Prince should have been the supreme moment of the Wilsons' social lives, confirmation of their position among East Yorkshire's elite families. Arthur was regarded as a man of taste and standing in the community, a business leader who lived up completely to his family's motto – 'Business first and everything else afterwards.' Like her husband, Mary Wilson enjoyed the respect and admiration of her peers. She had a reputation as a superb hostess with an eye for detail as well as a socialite with a flair for style.

Ironically, their impressive 60-room mansion had not been the original choice to host the Prince's party. Instead, the plan had been to use the Brantinghamthorpe home of Christopher Sykes, an East Riding MP and a member of a wealthy and well-established farming family based in Sledmere, near Driffield. Sykes had cared little for agriculture as a young man, preferring instead the high life in London and other fashionable spots across Europe as part of the Prince's inner circle of friends. In this role, he spent a small fortune entertaining the Prince only to be regarded as a figure of ridicule as he became ever more desperate to ingratiate himself. On one occasion, the notoriously badly behaved Prince emptied a glass of brandy over his head in front of guests only for Sykes to reply, 'As your Royal Highness pleases.' It quickly became a catchphrase in royal circles and was used as an excuse time and again to heap further humiliation on Sykes. In another incident, the Prince even stubbed a cigar out on his favourite stooge.

The MP appeared unperturbed by such put-downs and continued his lavish spending on entertaining the Prince and his friends with regular dinner parties both in East Yorkshire and London. However, by the time of the St. Leger meeting at Doncaster in September 1890 he had run into severe financial problems and simply couldn't afford to host another extravagant royal visit. His Brantinghamthorpe home was up for sale in a desperate bid to pay off some of his debts.

For the Wilsons, their offer to step into the breach meant they had truly arrived in the upper echelons of Victorian society. The Prince's son, Prince Albert Victor, had stayed at Tranby Croft the year before and Arthur Wilson had already met the heir to the throne during a previous visit to the East Riding in his capacity as Master of the Holderness Hunt. To make the occasion more memorable, it was decided that, as well as the Prince, a number of his close friends should be invited too. Arthur Wilson spared no expense for the visit, right down to providing a red carpet long enough to stretch the full length of the platform at Hessle railway station for the arrival of the Prince and his friends. He greeted the Prince personally at the station together with Christopher Sykes, who should have been the host but was now a guest.

A 14-course dinner followed by a short musical performance on the first evening was carefully planned and executed by the Wilsons, but the Prince wanted a little more excitement than that and suggested a game of baccarat. The game was said to be one of the Prince's favourites, its appeal probably heightened by the fact that under the era's strict gambling laws it was actually still illegal in England. The suggestion also caused a problem for Arthur Wilson as he had previously banned the game at Tranby Croft after his son Jack and a group of friends had been caught playing it for high stakes on a previous occasion.

With this in mind, Arthur realised that if he were to allow the game

The houseparty, outside Tranby Croft, including the Prince of Wales (later Edward VII) the day before the Baccarat Scandal.

with the Prince to go ahead, his previous orders to his own family and household would appear meaningless. Equally, could he refuse the future King of England? Faced with this difficult dilemma he chose to leave the room where preparations for the game were starting. The Prince, as usual, had prevailed and the game went ahead using the Prince's own special counters made of Russian leather and carrying his three feathers emblem. The counters went with him whenever he was invited to stay in the home of one of his circle of friends.

During that first evening's game, Jack Wilson noticed that one of the players, Sir William Gordon-Cumming, was apparently trying to increase his stake after being dealt a hand of cards, by dropping extra counters on top of his original bet. After the game Mary Wilson was told what had happened by her son. Anxious that a scandal had to be avoided at whatever cost, she ordered him to keep his mouth shut.

It proved to be an instruction that Jack largely ignored. By the following morning he had not only informed another guest, an Army officer called Berkeley Levett, but his own brother-in-law, Edward Lycett Green, who promptly told his wife Ethel. On the second night, there were further suspicions that Gordon-Cumming had cheated. At the end of the evening, his combined winnings were £228, a trivial sum compared to the wealth of those around the table and a drop in the ocean for a man who owned 40,000 acres of land in Scotland. Like Christopher Sykes, Gordon-Cumming was also well-known in society circles. The 42-year-old Lieutenant Colonel in the 1st Battalion Scots Guards was described by one newspaper of the day as 'possibly the handsomest man in London and possibly the rudest'. A notorious womaniser, he was regarded as one of the Prince's most trusted friends and had accompanied him on the train journey to Hessle station.

The growing gossip surrounding the two baccarat sessions plunged the Wilson household into a turmoil made worse on that second night by the sudden death of Mary's brother Henry, at his home in Hull. The family immediately went into mourning and the Royal party attended the following day's racing at Doncaster wearing black ties and arm-bands as a mark of respect, but the chain of events surrounding the baccarat games was now starting to spin out of control. Returning to Tranby Croft, the rumours had spread to more members of the party, and it was decided to act before the guests gathered again for dinner. Answering a knock on his room door, Gordon-Cumming was confronted by two senior members of the Prince's party, both of whom had not been present during the earlier baccarat sessions. They told him of the suspicions that he had cheated and that the Prince would have to be informed. Gordon-Cumming was stunned and angry. He strenuously denied cheating and said the very thought of it was an insult. He demanded to see the Prince himself and took the opportunity to again vehemently deny any misbehaviour. In Victorian high society, the accusation of cheating – particularly in the presence of royalty – was akin to the worst of possible crimes. A gentleman's honour and reputation could be ruined by such a slur.

Accordingly, those present over the two previous evenings at Tranby Croft decided on the time-honoured course of action favoured by the good and great in such circumstances and duly organised a cover-up. Despite his continued protests of innocence, Gordon-Cumming was presented with a statement to sign during his meeting with the Prince in a bid by those present to keep a lid on the potential scandal.

The statement read: 'In consideration of the promise made by the gentlemen whose names are subscribed to preserve silence with reference to an accusation which has been made with regard to my conduct at baccarat on the nights of Monday and Tuesday, the 8th and 9th September 1890, at Tranby Croft, I will on my part solemnly undertake never to play cards again as long as I live.'

Gordon-Cumming faced a dilemma over the statement. Were he to sign it, he would, in effect, be branding himself a cheat. If he refused, then word would almost certainly get about and he would be ruined anyway. Despite continuing to deny any wrongdoing he duly signed. Months later his signature was to be viewed by a jury as an admission of guilt.

Any hopes of keeping the incident under wraps proved fruitless as the story inevitably leaked out. Some have attributed this to Lady Brooke, a society beauty and notorious gossip, who was the Prince's mistress at the time. Although not present at Tranby Croft, she was popularly believed to have relayed the events there to London's chattering classes at a later date, thereby living up to her unflattering nickname of Babbling Brooke. There would also be a suggestion that relations between the Prince and Gordon-Cumming had soured just prior to leaving London for the St

Sir William Gordon-Cumming.

Leger meeting, after the latter had been allegedly caught in a romantic tryst with Lady Brooke. Another story at the time suggested the allegations were already a talking point at Doncaster racecourse on the afternoon following the party's first evening at Tranby Croft.

Hoping the secret pact would hold, Gordon-Cumming did his best to stay out of the public eye by dividing his time between his Scottish estate, his regiment and his private members' club in Paris. However an anonymous letter posted from the French capital four months after that fateful card game in Anlaby informed him that gossips across the continent's social hotspots were busy swapping tales about the affair and his role in it.

Enraged by what he viewed as a betrayal, Gordon-Cumming attempted to restore his increasingly battered reputation by suing some of the signatories to his statement for defamation. He suspected at least one, maybe more, had deliberately gone back on their word by revealing details of the cheating allegations against him. The Prince was not among those being sued but he would be required as a witness in the resulting court case. By then, a military enquiry had already been launched but any hearing was put on hold until after the civil action being brought over the case. The move would trigger Gordon-Cumming's ultimate downfall and provide an unprecedented court case for the public to get their teeth into.

The case was heard by Lord Coleridge, the Lord Chief Justice of England, and featured eight defendants, including Jack Wilson, Edward Lycett Green, Berkeley Levett, and George Coventry, the ninth Earl of Coventry. It quickly became a society spectacle with contemporary reports faithfully recording every aristocratic arrival and departure from the courtroom in much the same way grand society events were covered by the newspapers. The Prince was apparently reluctant to testify, no doubt recalling a previous court appearance during a divorce case in 1870 when he denied having an affair with Lady Mourdant, the young wife of Sir Charles Mourdant. However, he was forced into the witness box again when Gordon-Cumming's barrister invoked Army regulations requiring an officer to report the illegal actions of a fellow officer. As an officer himself, the Prince admitted under cross-examination that he hadn't done so, while acknowledging his own participation in the events at Tranby Croft, including the public revelation of his penchant for card-playing.

Although seemingly innocuous by today's moral standards, his self-confessed love of gambling was viewed with alarm by large sections of

An early photographic portrait of the Prince of Wales (later Edward VII), c.1880.

late Victorian society. As one newspaper put it: 'The testimony taken today brought out the first really important disclosure in regard to the Prince of Wales, for it is admitted on all sides that the more conservative and religious subjects of the Queen will be far from pleased to hear that the heir apparent has been in the habit of carrying a baccarat set about with him while paying visits to the country houses of his friends.'

Apart from his brief spell in the witness box, the Prince spent the rest of the proceedings sitting in a red velvet armchair next to the Lord Chief Justice. Some observers would suggest any hope of a fair hearing for Gordon-Cumming was fatally undermined simply because of this peculiar seating arrangement. While the Prince's own evidence was quite bland it did add to the tide turning against Gordon-Cumming, despite the pair being close friends over the years. The latter had even put his London house at the Prince's disposal for a series of supposedly secret flings with girlfriends.

The most dramatic evidence came from Jack Wilson. Confident and assured despite being much younger than his fellow defendants, he gave a detailed account of the alleged cheating in his own evidence and then backed it up under a tough cross-examination by Sir Edward Clarke, the

The scene in court.

9

Solicitor General, who was representing Gordon-Cumming. He told the court: 'When I gave the order to change the tables after the disclosures of the first night's play I was ready to stake my life that Sir William Gordon-Cumming cheated. I and my mother sat down to play on the second night believing that the chalk line which we had marked on the table would prevent any further attempt to cheat. On the second night I noticed there was something wrong with Sir William Gordon-Cumming twenty minutes after the beginning of play. Lady Coventry was sitting between the plaintiff and General Owen Williams. I sat around the corner. The plaintiff did not put his hands over the line until he knew that his own side had won and then he put over a £10 counter, making his stake £15 instead of £5.' Sir Edward Clarke then asked why Wilson had not raised an objection to this apparent sleight of hand. 'Because there were ladies present and it would have been an ungentlemanly thing to have had a row before them,' he replied.

Clarke's closing speech to the jury was the sensation the packed public gallery had been hoping for. In it, he dismissed the Wilsons as ill-mannered nouveaux riches, suggested the two evenings at Tranby Croft had been awash with alcohol and claimed Gordon-Cumming had only signed the statement to help avoid his old friend the Prince of Wales being dragged into a public scandal. He even took a hefty swipe at the Prince himself. After reminding the jury of the reputation-threatening risk facing Gordon-Cumming of being dismissed by the Army, he went on: 'I wish to say in unmistakable terms that it would be impossible for the authorities to do any such thing and leave on that list the names of Field Marshal the Prince of Wales and General Owen Williams.'

The suggestion that the future King should be thrown out of the Army brought gasps from the public gallery but Clarke saved his best until last. Addressing the jury he said, 'It is too late to undo much of the mischief that has been done.' Then he turned directly to face the Prince and after a deliberately lengthy pause continued, 'and it may be too late to save the reputation of some people mentioned in this case but,' he paused again turning back to the jury, 'it is not too late for you to prevent the completion of the sacrifice of this gallant officer.'

When he finished, the court erupted in spontaneous applause and cheering but the Lord Chief Justice was not impressed. 'Silence! This is not a theatre!' He roared.

His summing up the next day was regarded by most observers to be hugely one-sided and very much against Gordon-Cumming, perhaps reflecting the proximity of the Prince of Wales sitting alongside him. Eventually, the jury deliberated for just over ten minutes before finding in favour of Gordon-Cumming's original accusers.

It was not a popular decision. In the courtroom there were hisses and boos aimed at the jurors from the public gallery, while some spectators surged forward and tried to attack some of the defendants. The Wilson family eventually had to be steered through an empty court to a side exit from the building to avoid the hostile crowd. Most of the prominent newspapers of the day had also sided with Gordon-Cumming, with public opinion frowning on the behaviour of the playboy Prince and his associates. The class-ridden snobbery of the day was also much in evidence, with the Wilsons being widely criticised for attempting to act above their social status. Despite their undoubted wealth and an enviable track record of charitable work in the Hull area, certain sections of the landed aristocracy still regarded them as vulgar, money-flaunting types all too eager to buy their way to the top.

As a result of the scandal, Gordon-Cumming was dismissed from the Army the day after the trial and retired in disgrace to his Scottish estate. On the same day as his dismissal he married Florence Garner, an American heiress who had supported him throughout the case. Ostracised from high society, he remained bitter over the affair until his death in 1930.

As for the Prince of Wales, he stopped playing baccarat altogether, although he continued to gamble in a more discreet fashion. He also parted company with the loose-lipped Lady Brooke, replacing her with a new mistress, Alice Keppel.

For their part, the Wilsons never entertained the Prince again but they continued to enjoy his support. Shortly before the trial Jack Wilson was admitted to the exclusive Marlborough Club in London on the Prince's recommendation, while other members of the Royal family continued to pay visits to the Wilson home in Anlaby.

Chapter 2

The Baronet and Lady Satin Tights

HOVERING ON THE BRINK of bankruptcy and unable to provide his usual lavish hospitality for the Princes of Wales, Christopher Sykes was one of the few guests at Tranby Croft to emerge from the Baccarat Scandal without any great stain on his name despite financial problems. Although present throughout, he was not involved in any of the card games, nor was he cited in William Gordon-Cumming's ill-fated legal action which would ultimately be played out in newspaper columns across the world. Some would argue that Sykes' reputation was already in tatters because of his mounting debts but he would eventually be eclipsed as a focus of high society scandal by his elder brother Tatton.

Like the Wilsons' beloved Tranby Croft, the ancestral home of the Sykes dynasty also owed its existence to wealth created via Hull's port. With Cumbrian origins dating back to the Middle Ages, the family arrived in the East Riding in the mid-16th century in the shape of William Sykes, who had already established himself as a successful cloth trader in West Yorkshire. The family knack for business eventually hit gold some 100 years later when Daniel Sykes began amassing a fortune through shipping and finance. He was succeeded by his son Richard, who diversified further, concentrating on the lucrative Baltic trade in imported pig iron. Through his first marriage to an heiress, Richard divided his time between the family business in Hull and a new home in Sledmere, but it was to be his son, also called Richard, who decided to build Sledmere Hall in an ambitious development project which included the planting of 20,000 trees.

Richard died without an heir and the estate passed first to his brother Mark and then to his nephew, Mark's only surviving son, Christopher. He switched the family focus from merchant trading to agriculture, selling off the Sykes' interests in shipping and finance, and with the help of two large inheritances embarked on ambitious plans to enclose huge areas of land for farming.

Until then, the Yorkshire Wolds had largely been one vast, uncultivated stretch of open space, unmarked by hedges or ditches. Sir Christopher's vision to bring this chalk-scarred pasture land under his ownership and convert it into productive, well-drained farmland became a benchmark for others to follow across the country. At the same time, he also built two new wings to the hall and completely landscaped the grounds, while supervising the relocation of most of the adjacent village to fit in with his plans. It was visionary stuff and within 30 years he had masterminded the transformation of largely barren land mostly populated by individual sheep farmers into a hugely productive and profitable agricultural estate with an emphasis on corn growing.

As one contemporary historian wrote: 'The pages of history have blazoned the deeds of heroes who, in the career of ambition and conquest, have subdued and desolated the fertile provinces; but how much more dignified in character, in the eye of reason, is he who clothes the land with the beauties of a new creation, converts the barren wastes into fertile regions and diffuses peace, plenty and cheerfulness through an extensive district!'

His work was eventually continued by his son Tatton, the fourth baronet in the family lineage and arguably the most famous. Born in 1772, Sir Tatton would become one of the best-known Yorkshiremen of his day, but he did not inherit the estate and his title until 1823 on the death of his elder brother Mark, who had initially succeeded their father after his death some 22 years earlier. Sir Mark was more interested in politics and literature than farming, serving as MP for York for quarter of a century until retiring due to ill-health. At the same time he amassed one of the finest private libraries in England, filling parts of the hall with numerous first editions of classic books along with valuable manuscripts, rare examples of 15th-century printing and volumes of Elizabethan poetry.

Tatton Sykes was very different from his brother, a fact underlined by his decision just a few months after Sir Mark's death to put most of his literary collection up for sale. The sale raised £16,000 and a large part of the library's rarest works were acquired by another devoted bibliophile, Thomas Grenville, who was also a trustee of the British Museum. As such, many of the treasures collected by Sir Mark would eventually become part of the country's rarest literary possessions by way of Grenville's own later bequest.

Young Tatton Sykes was educated at Westminster School in London but was not a natural scholar. His father tried to suggest a legal career as an option and secured an articled clerk's position for him with a firm in the capital. However, his interest waned and instead he was found another job in a Hull bank. Bored with office work and hankering for the countryside, he eventually returned to Sledmere and started working with his father on the family's farming estate.

He developed a flair for sheep farming and stock breeding, playing a leading role in organising what would become his own annual sheep sales while travelling around the country to buy and sell animals at other sales. He also continued his father's work in pioneering new agricultural techniques and was credited with being the first to discover the value of bones in the making of manure, having spotted the grass growing outside his kennels was much healthier than elsewhere and that it was also the spot where his dogs ate and buried their bones. He even visited Sheffield to buy waste bone-dust from the city's famous knife-handle makers to provide the raw materials for his own manure and built his own bone-crushing machine to grind out the raw materials he required. Initially few believed the traditional muck heap would ever be replaced by his invention but eventually bone-meal would become a common ingredient in plant food.

However, his real passion was horses, and by the time he became the fourth baronet on the death of his brother he was one of the country's leading breeders of horse-racing bloodstock. At his peak, he owned literally hundreds of horses, and the Sledmere Stud, as it became known, was regarded as the largest of its kind in Britain and possibly even the world.

As a horseman, Sir Tatton's exploits in the saddle were the stuff of legend. One tale involved him riding to Aberdeen from Sledmere, with his racing jacket under his waistcoat and a clean shirt and razor in his pocket. After winning the race in Scotland, he then rode back to Doncaster to watch the annual St Leger meeting in a carefully planned four-day journey. For some 40 years he was also Master of the Holderness Hunt, meeting all the kennel expenses from his own purse.

His horsemanship and a youthful background in boxing, having studied the sport at close quarters with two of the era's noted pugilists, Gentleman Jackson and Jem Belcher, ensured his reputation as a man's man. A popular story surrounding one of his visits to a sheep sale involved an incident in a village pub, where a burly cattle-drover grabbed Sykes'

A portrait of Sir Tatton Sykes of Sledmere, in his 90th year, reflecting his reputation as a horseman.

pitcher of beer and gulped it down, much to the amusement of a companion. Tatton said nothing and then quietly asked for another drink only for the second drover to seize it and dispatch it in a similar fashion. A third pint was ordered without any repeat but when Tatton had finished his drink he ordered the first drover to stand up and duly floored him with a single punch. He then turned to the second man and laid him out too before leaving the pub.

Inheriting Sledmere on the death of his brother, Tatton was 50-years-old and still a bachelor. Concerned about identifying a potential heir and with no thoughts about marriage himself, he suggested that his sister's only son Mark should marry a cousin called Mary Foulis. When the young man declined to go along with his uncle's plans, Tatton astonished his family by proposing to Mary instead. Despite his age, the couple went on to have eight children – two sons and six daughters – but Lady Sykes made little attempt to change her husband's set ways. Her own escape from his strict routine as a country squire engrossed with horses and the estate was developing the gardens around the house and spending much of her time in the family's huge home in central London, where she become known as a society hostess, entertaining the likes of the Duke of Wellington at the height of his popularity.

Although enormously wealthy, Tatton preferred to live a simple life. Ignoring the fashionable lure and convenience of the railway, he would invariably opt to travel by horse, once riding to London and back to sit for a portrait by the artist Sir Francis Grant. Accompanied by a servant, he covered around 40 miles day despite being 80-years-old at the time. Fine food would be shunned in favour of a Spartan diet, while he stuck rigidly to one style of dress throughout his long adult life – a long frock-coat, drab breeches, a frilled shirt and boots.

While his dress sense owed more to the fashions of a century earlier, at home he lived up to the stereotype of the severely strict Victorian father, literally ruling the roost with a rod of iron. One relative later wrote: 'His pleasant Adamesque house was a barbaric hell. He ruled over his family with the vicious rage of a stone-age tyrant. On them he imposed simple and intolerable rules of life; that the virtues resided in rising at dawn in winter and summer, on no hot water, on no creature comforts and on frequent applications of the paternal whip.

'When his sons returned from the squalor of school, they were often greeted with flagellations which must have made them sigh for the birches of Harrow; on one occasion the discipline was administered because, on unpacking, the unmanly frippery of tooth brushes was discovered among their effects.

'The elder boy, being the weaker of the two, was treated with special concern. The heroic old father was once seen armed with a whip driving the child barefoot and screaming down the drive.'

The fact that the two sons – Tatton and Christopher – would grow up to be very different characters from their father was probably no surprise.

Christopher, the younger, virtually turned his back on Sledmere to become a fashionable young dandy caught up in the whirl of London's high society and eventually a long-standing member of the Prince of Wales' party-going set. His brush with national notoriety courtesy of the Tranby House Affair came late in his life and two years after he retired from one of the most undistinguished political careers ever witnessed at Westminster. In 24 years as a Conservative MP representing three different East Riding constituencies he made only six speeches in the House of Commons and gave strong personal support to just one piece of legislation – a bill which established official protection for wild seabirds and their eggs. Some opponents claimed his parliamentary days should have ended earlier than they actually did after he lost his seat in the Buckrose constituency by a single vote in the 1886 General Election to Liberal challenger William McArthur. Sykes and his Conservative supporters refused to accept the result and lodged an appeal claiming there had been a miscount of the votes recorded. Their petition was the subject of a special hearing in York, which reversed the decision and declared Sykes the winner by 11 votes.

His older brother Tatton had inherited the baronetcy in 1862 after the death of 92-year-old Sir Tatton, an event marked by public mourning across the Wolds on a scale normally reserved for members of Royalty. The new Sir Tatton was abroad at the time, developing what would be a lifelong passion for foreign travel and an escape route of his own from the tortured childhood he experienced for much of the time at Sledmere at the hand of his father. Often venturing abroad alone since he was painfully shy in the company of others, he was nonetheless one of the most travelled men of his generation when news reached him of his father's death, having visited places as far flung as China, Russia, Mexico and Japan.

Six months later he followed in his father's footsteps by conducting a huge sale at Sledmere. Instead of his late uncle's library going under the hammer, it was old Tatton's entire stud, an event described by one newspaper as 'the most remarkable sale of bloodstock which ever took place in this or any other country'. The idea behind the three-day sale was to make a clean sweep of things in more ways than one.

The stud had mushroomed under old Tatton, with an emphasis on quantity rather than quality, and his son was determined to start afresh and create a leaner but ultimately more successful breeding business. It also provided the perfect opportunity to stamp his own mark on Sledmere at the expense of his father's memory. His other move was to dig up the gardens around the house and dismantle the orangery where his mother would grow plants. He even went as far as ploughing the immaculate lawns right to the walls of the house and issued strict orders that cultivating flowers in the village was now banned, declaring them to be 'nasty, untidy things'.

It is highly likely that Sir Tatton suffered from a form of obsessive compulsive disorder. When a friend remarked how some of the shrub gardens around the grounds would be improved with patches of flowers planted in front of them, he reportedly replied, 'No! No! No! I like to see the ground raked over, raked over, raked over.' Repeating phrases over and over was another habit he found difficult to shake off.

His odd behaviour came to define his character and many simply regarded him as eccentric, a view underlined by an insistence that everyone living in cottages belonging to the Sledmere estate should refrain from using their front doors. To prevent them doing so he insisted that every front door should be locked and bolted at all times, with new cottages being built without any front doors at all. Some said it was because he disliked the sight of women gossiping on their doorsteps, others suggested it was down to his view that children should not be allowed to play in the street and should only be permitted to play in back yards where no one could see them.

Sir Tatton was also obsessed with his own rather fragile health. A weak child, he grew up convinced that a daily diet of milk pudding was the best way to ward off stomach ailments. Even on his travels abroad he would always ensure supplies of milk pudding were plentiful, often taking his own cook with him just to prepare his favourite dish.

He also believed good health was only possible by maintaining a constant body temperature. Having spent much of his time in China and Japan, he favoured the more temperate climates of the Far East and replicated this back home by wearing several different coloured overcoats at the same time. During a rare visit to Ascot races, he embarrassed his brother Christopher in front of the Prince of Wales by turning up wearing his collection of specially made overcoats. 'Who is that extraordinary-looking fellow over there?' asked the Prince, gesturing towards Sir Tatton. 'Why on earth do they allow people in the enclosure in such ridiculous clothes?' It could have been worse for he was also known to wear two pairs of trousers and once startled passengers on a train by removing his socks and shoes when he got too hot, before sticking his feet out of the window.

The one thing he shared with his father was an apparent lack of interest in the opposite sex. With an estate of 36,000 acres and an income to match, he was certainly qualified as an eligible bachelor but his eccentricities meant that few considered the 48-year-old would ever marry. Prudence Cavendish-Bentinck, the wife of a prominent Tory MP, had other ideas.

She was determined to find a suitably wealthy husband for her daughter Jessica, not least because the two frequently clashed. A marriage was viewed as the perfect excuse to bring the strong-willed girl under the controlling influence of an aristocratic husband who would ensure she was provided for. When the Cavendish-Bentincks happened to meet Sir Tatton during a family holiday in Bavaria in the summer of 1874, Prudence quickly made it her business to establish his credentials as a suitable husband-to-be for Jessica. Aware of his reputation as a recluse, she engineered a supposedly chance meeting between the pair by deliberately allowing her daughter to become separated from the family party. She knew that Sir Tatton alone would come to her daughter's assistance and, being a gentleman, that he would also accompany her safely back to the family. When he did so Prudence pretended to be angry at the thought of her daughter being on her own for a whole night and took the charade one step further on their return to England by accusing Sir Tatton of compromising the girl. Shocked by the very thought of any wrong-doing, he fell headlong into his future mother-in-law's trap by proposing marriage as a way of avoiding any potential scandal. Aged just 18 years old, Jessica was about to become the next Lady Sykes.

The 30-year age gap between bride and groom was politely overlooked in the historic surroundings of Westminster Abbey that same summer, when the couple married in what was described in some newspapers as 'The Wedding of the Season'.

However, it soon became clear that it was a spectacularly ill-matched union. Jessica was an extrovert with a talent for languages and art. A keen interest in travel was just about the only passion she shared with her new husband. It later emerged he took six months to consummate their marriage and, even then, only in the clumsiest manner possible. At Sledmere, Jessica tried and failed to change Sir Tatton's set ways while becoming more removed from the social circles in London she had

The engagement photograph of Sir Tatton Sykes, 5th Baronet, and Jessie. (Reproduced by kind permission of Christopher S. Sykes).

previously enjoyed. Persuading him to rent a flat in the capital where she could entertain during the social season was one concession she won from him. True to form, he stayed in East Yorkshire while she headed south.

During this part of his life, Sir Tatton embarked on a personal mission to restore over 15 churches scattered across East Yorkshire, spending a small fortune from his own resources to fund the work. Inspired by the religious devotion witnessed during his early travels abroad, he set about trying to replicate that demonstration of faith in his home county. The arrival of the couple's only son, Mark, in early 1879, brought brief hope they could forge a lasting relationship, but within three years Jessica turned to religion for strength in the face of her crumbling marriage and converted to the Catholic Church along with her son Mark. Sir Tatton's restoration programme had involved local Church of England properties, but that didn't stop Jessica lobbying him hard to fund and build a new

Catholic cathedral in London. Fortunately for his finances, he eventually declined.

Her religious conversion mirrored a growing enthusiasm for charitable causes. In both East Yorkshire and London she became known for her extreme generosity and compassion. Food, clothes and money were regularly donated to families in need, and in Hull her work among the poor living in appalling slum housing conditions made her extremely popular. The Lady Sykes' Christmas Treat established itself as an important annual event in the city, providing poor families with festive presents carefully chosen by her ladyship. In London she would live the high life, attending a series of fashionable balls and concerts, and then astonish her upper-crust contemporaries by rising early each morning to carry out charity work through her connections with the Catholic church or visit a girls' school she had helped establish with the help of Sir Tatton's wealth. Such kindness and compassion earned her the nickname among the poor of Lady Bountiful. Among her upper-class contemporaries, however, she was known by another less flattering nickname – Lady Satin Tights.

The title was a play on her husband's name but also owed much to her increasingly wayward lifestyle on London's high society merry-go-round. Having persuaded him to rent a much grander house in the heart of fashionable Mayfair, Jessica developed a reputation for laying on wild entertainment in which she played a full part. Behaving exactly as she pleased, she smoked, drank and gambled with enthusiasm alongside a series of regular guests who not only reflected her love of cosmopolitan life but also shared her passions for literature, travel and adventure. In contrast, her husband who rarely drank and frowned on anyone who smoked, usually managed to find any excuse to stay well away from London's fun and games by remaining in Sledmere.

In 1890 Jessica embarked on a typically passionate affair with ambitious diplomat Jack Gorst while on holiday in Egypt with Sir Tatton and Mark. As Sir Eldon Gorst, Jack would later become Consul-General in Cairo overseeing the British occupation and control over the Suez Canal, while his younger sister Edith would eventually marry Jessica and Sir Tatton's only son Mark.

Jack and Jessica's brief relationship lasted two eventful years. When her drinking and the increasingly promiscuous behaviour which accompanied it became more than he could bear, he decided to end their affair. In his remarkably candid diaries, he recorded their lovemaking with a series of noughts and crosses, tallying the score at the end of each year. Later, recalling their affair, he wrote: 'She exercised a great influence over my life for the next two years and undoubtedly contributed very largely to the formation of my character and general views during that period. Some years older than myself, she possessed great intelligence coupled with an extraordinary variety of knowledge and a force of character unusual in one of her sex. All these qualities made her in those days a most delightful and instructive companion.'

The darker side to Jessica's personality took over once their relationship came to an end, with Gorst admitting in his diary that 'popular rumour' about his lover's 'terrible failing' had been true all along – her drinking and gambling were now becoming uncontrollable. She began running up huge losses on the gambling tables at fashionable parties. Even worse, she started to become a familiar punter at a number of bookmakers' shops. With unpaid bills piling up, a recently appointed accountant at Sledmere discovered she had been drawing on the estate account to fund her betting sprees and advised Sir Tatton to refuse any further pleas for money.

With her grip on financial reality loosening by the day, Jessica turned to moneylenders charging exorbitant interest rates to raise funds and also started dabbling unsuccessfully on the Stock Market. Her relationship with her son Mark also became strained after she asked him to consider making her a loan from his own allowance. When he too was advised to refuse to go along with her request, she then made a fruitless attempt to see if her son could persuade his father to change his mind over halting her access to any more money from the Sledmere coffers.

While his father remained a distant figure throughout his childhood, young Mark had been close to his mother until sent to Beaumont College, a private school in Berkshire, at the age of ten. For the next five years he would come to dread visits by Jessica, fearing she would turn up at the school either drunk or hung over. Embarrassing scenes involving his mother and played out in front of his contemporaries became commonplace.

In 1896, two years after Jessica had removed Mark from Beaumont to send him to another private Jesuit school in Monaco, her faltering marriage to Sir Tatton imploded in spectacular fashion. Driven into a rage over her increasingly exacting behaviour, he lost all self-control and had all the Sledmere terriers hanged. The strain on the introverted eccentric who shunned the limelight was such that he eventually decided to take legal advice on how to manage Jessica's spiralling debts. The solution proposed by his solicitors was dramatic and unprecedented.

The 1870 Married Woman's Property Act had for the first time allowed a married woman to keep her earnings by establishing that any money she made whether through a wage, investment, gift or inheritance was classed as separate property from that of her husband. The act is regarded as one of the first significant steps towards women's right to vote, but it also contained an amendment which allowed aggrieved husbands to free themselves of all debts incurred by their wives without having to resort to a divorce. The legislation required the husband to publish a newspaper notice effectively renouncing any responsibility for monies owed by his partner. Such a public admission was considered almost unthinkable in polite society where appearances mattered, but Sir Tatton decided he had no alternative and on 7 December 1896 he became the first person in Britain to publish such a notice, choosing the columns of *The Times* newspaper to lay bare the true state of his marriage for the world to see.

The notice, which was repeated a week later in the same newspaper, read: 'I, Sir Tatton Sykes, Baronet of Sledmere in the county of York, and 46 Grosvenor Street in the county of London, hereby give notice that I will not be responsible for any debts or engagements which my wife Lady Jessica Christina Sykes may contract, whether purporting to be on my behalf or by my authority or otherwise.'

However humiliating the decision to publish the notice must have been, it did the trick for Sir Tatton, as Jessica's creditors turned their attentions away from the Sledmere estate and instead demanded payment from her. The move forced her to sign an agreement with her husband under which he paid her £12,000 to discharge her immediate debts and guaranteed a further £5,000 a year to cover future receipts, along with a fixed sum to pay all her household and stabling costs in London. In return, she promised not to gamble on the money markets or to bet for credit on the turf.

The deal didn't last long as massive secret debts Jessica had kept hidden from her husband at the time came back to haunt her as more creditors started appearing out of the woodwork. After Sir Tatton refused her any more funds above the level set in the agreement she filed for divorce, only to abandon her legal action when she discovered she would not get as much alimony as she first believed she was entitled to.

Just over two years after the notices appeared in *The Times,* events reached a new low when a moneylender called Daniel Jay brought a court action against Sir Tatton and Lady Jessica to recover £15,870 resulting from five promissory notes which he claimed had been signed by both of them. Heard in London's High Court, the case predictably attracted a storm of publicity, not least because of the odd couple at the centre of it all. Jessica admitted her liability but claimed her husband had not only signed the notes pledging investment in Alaskan gold mining stocks but played a full part in their commissioning. Sir Tatton, on the other hand, denied signing or knowing anything about the notes and maintained the signatures were forgeries.

The packed public gallery lapped it all up, particularly when Lady Jessica attempted to present her husband as a figure of ridicule. 'We were speaking only yesterday,' she told the court at one point during her evidence. 'I hoped he would be better advised, and wear his greatcoat in court because of draughts.' With laughter still echoing around the room, she went on to claim they had never had a cross word between them in their lives. One of young Mark Sykes' tutors was even called as a witness to testify the signatures were genuine and that, in his opinion, Sir Tatton was clearly insane because of his habit of wearing seven overcoats at the same time.

Backed by a number of hand-writing experts and his own bank manager, who vouched the signatures were not Sir Tatton's, the 72-year-old won the upper hand by presenting a more plausible case than his wife, who claimed his mean-minded ways with money had forced her to run up huge debts just to keep Sledmere and their London home running. He also suggested that early in their marriage Jessica had forged his signature on the lease of the house in Grosvenor Street to secure its possession, and that ever since she had continued to forge his signature on any number of documents to obtain funds, while he simply went along with it because he could not face an argument with her.

The case lasted five days before the jury returned its verdict in favour of Sir Tatton, ruling he had not signed the promissory notes and that they were forgeries created one way or another by his wife. Vindicated, he returned to a much quieter life in Sledmere, while Jessica gave up the house in Grosvenor Street and moved into another London property left to her in the will of her brother-in-law Christopher. She tried to reform her ways by giving up gambling and cutting down on her drinking while forging a new career as a writer, but despite the age gap between them, she failed to outlive Sir Tatton, dying in 1912 after a series of seizures. At a memorial service held at Westminster Cathedral, the chosen text was appropriately titled 'Charity covers a multitude of sins'.

Sir Tatton's final exit also mirrored his eccentric character. A year later he died while staying at the Metropole Hotel in London. Worried about the impact of the news on his guests, the hotel manager wanted to smuggle the body out of the premises in a hollowed-out sofa until Mark Sykes intervened. 'However my father leaves this hotel, he leaves it like a gentleman,' he told the manager, before arranging a more suitable mode of transport. Back at Sledmere, his father had left instructions to be carried to his grave on the estate in a farm-cart.

Chapter 3

Power, Corruption and Bribes

SOME 20 MILES from central Glasgow, the Scottish coastal town of Helensburgh is an unlikely setting for what was a shocking end to one of the most dramatic and tragic chapters in the story of Hull's great scandals.

Today it appeals to commuters and tourists alike, lying on the north side of the Firth of Clyde, between Gare Loch to the west and the southernmost tip of Loch Lomond to the east. But on a cold March night in 1932, the town proved to be the final, fateful destination of a former Hull politician facing the prospect of both personal and professional ruin.

At the time, Albert Digby Willoughby was one of the best known figures in Hull, but in Helensburgh he was just another guest signing in for the night at a boarding-house on one of the town's main streets. When a member of staff went to his room the next morning, he was found dead. The room itself was full of gas. Any suggestion of foul play was ruled out almost immediately and, although the police in Helensburgh subsequently declined to give details about personal papers and documents found in the hotel room, it was widely accepted that Willoughby had committed suicide.

His health had undoubtedly been poor in the months leading up to his death. A heart problem had been diagnosed and he had only just returned from a cruise on the White Star liner *S.S. Laurentic*. The trip was meant to act as a health tonic but, according to one fellow passenger who met him onboard, it ended up having the opposite effect. 'He was an ill man who never complained,' the travelling companion told a newspaper after his death. 'In many talks with him I discovered how badly he suffered from indigestion and insomnia. He never seemed to eat and drank nothing more stimulating than water. He was depressed towards the end of the voyage in that the improvement in health he had anticipated had not materialised and when we arrived in London he went straight to bed.' The one impression Willoughby did leave on his fellow traveller was of a man still hugely proud of his achievements in civic life in his home city. 'He talked animatedly and with deep feeling, chiefly of Hull and its civic achievements and the future development of the city of which he was intensely proud,' he recalled.

There is little doubt that Willoughby was passionate about Hull and that he played a significant role in the expansion of the city in the early decades of the 20th century, when the power and influence of local government in the form of the Hull Corporation was at its height. However, as in similar scandals, that same heady cocktail of power and influence also proved to be his downfall. For some it inspires greatness, with Willoughby it triggered greed, manipulation and ultimately corruption.

Born in Brook Street in 1879, he spent his childhood growing up in the heart of the rapidly expanding city centre. After spending a few years in London he returned home and started work as a tailor, opening a shop in Charles Street. He later switched to selling perfumes and by the time he moved to new premises in Jameson Street he was specialising in toys and fancy goods.

Willoughby entered Hull's municipal arena in 1914 when he was elected to the Corporation as a representative for Botanic Ward, and over the next 18 years he carved out a reputation for being one of the most controversial councillors in the Guildhall. A staunch Conservative, he was a dynamic and forceful personality who threw himself into the work of the authority. Almost immediately after his election he became chairman of a committee overseeing food rationing in relation to the war effort. Later he carried out a similar role overseeing the control of coal stocks in the city.

His elevation through the political ranks at the Guildhall was swift. He was elected to what was then the still important title of Sheriff of the city in 1919 and became Lord Mayor five years later, using his year as the city's First Citizen to put forward a scheme proposing major changes to the many railway level crossings dissecting Hull's main roads at the time. His vision was for a series of bridges capable of carrying traffic over the crossings. It was a typical Willoughby idea – ambitious, potentially costly and probably ahead of its time. Rejection by the Government and then in a poll of ratepayers was a wound he carried with him for the rest of his political career.

Transport remained one of his great passions and he was to play a central role in two defining projects which can still be seen today. As chairman of the Bridges Committee, he was instrumental in securing a vital £50,000 grant from the Government to build North Bridge across the River Hull. Later during his year as Lord Mayor, he also became one of the driving forces behind the development of Ferensway, the new city-centre street modelled on the Headrow in Leeds and some of London's grander thoroughfares. Partly built on land formerly occupied by some of Hull's worst slum housing, the ambitious dual carriageway was initially proposed to be called Quality Street, while Willoughby himself put forward proposals for a series of imposing mock-Tudor buildings lining the route from Paragon Station to Beverley Road. Both ideas were later shelved, with Willoughby's medieval concept attracting much ridicule from some colleagues and sections of the local press.

However, it was in his role as chairman of the Corporation's Tramways Committee that he would become one of the most controversial figures in local politics. By the time of the General Strike in May 1926 he had been in charge of the city's tram system for seven years, championing a steady

Digby Willoughby (second from left) pictured during a visit to Hull Kingston Rovers' Craven Park stadium in 1926 by the then Prince of Wales. Standing next to the Prince is Digby Willoughby's long-standing friend and political ally Frank Finn, Lord Mayor at the time.

expansion to the point where it was regarded as one of the finest of its kind outside London. The events of the strike, and the turbulent social upheaval that led up to it, tested his famously steely resolve to the limit.

With memories of the Russian Revolution still fresh in the mind, many establishment figures saw the industrial and political unrest of that spring as a real threat to democracy and their own previously untouchable power base. For the likes of Willoughby, there was only one way to counter a mass walk-out by tramway workers who, by their actions, threatened to bring the city to a standstill. In the teeth of fierce criticism both from his Labour opponents on the Corporation and sections of the public, he went out and recruited a volunteer workforce, including undergraduates from Oxford and Cambridge. When the strike was over, he fanned the flames by refusing to reinstate all of the original tram workers to their previous positions and insisted that any volunteers who wanted to remain working on the trams should be given priority.

Eventually, a compromise was reached allowing tram workers to return alongside volunteers, but a subsequent account of the events in the *Hull Daily Mail* manages to capture both the character of the man at the centre of a political crisis and the extraordinary tensions of the time: 'He proved himself a strong man when a strong man was needed. He won admiration on one side and obloquy on the other in the abnormal position which arose when the tramwaymen unexpectedly broke their agreement of service. As a citizen he claimed the right of the general public to a tram service. No one would possibly like to go again through the experiences of the dark week in May of 1926, and no one knows what the consequences of failure for the forces of discipline and order would have been.'

Following the General Strike and its messy aftermath, his Labour opponents on the Corporation started searching for a new opportunity to attack Willoughby. They didn't have to wait very long. Within months he was in the firing line again, this time accused of abusing his position as chief magistrate and, more importantly, as chairman of a committee entrusted with running the Guildhall's banqueting facilities, in the design of a new, large stained-glass window to be installed in the building's banqueting room. His critics might have been able to stomach the cost of the lavishly decorated window had it not included several references to Willoughby's own family. After protracted debates over what his enemies regarded as distasteful personal vanity, councillors eventually decided to drop them from the final version of the window's design.

In an era of unprecedented municipal power, Willoughby appeared to be immersed in the workings of the Corporation. To many he was the Corporation and at one time or another sat on every one of its committees, acting as chairman of some of the most powerful and influential. However, it was the way he manipulated this power that ultimately proved to be his undoing.

A year after he was first elected in 1914, rumours began to spread about councillors exploiting their positions on the Corporation for financial gain. Although no one was named publicly, suspicions grew that some councillors were acting as middlemen for other individuals or companies seeking deals or contracts with the Corporation.

In a nutshell, civic influence and inside knowledge was secretly being turned into private profit by the some of the very people elected to look after the public purse.

Whether Willoughby's arrival at the Corporation and the start of this speculation was coincidental is probably lost in the mists of time. However, a resolution ultimately adopted by the Corporation in November 1915 showed the level of concern over the allegations in some quarters. Moved by Labour councillor Benno Pearlman, it effectively banned any member from acting on behalf of any individual or company seeking to carry out any form of business transaction with the Corporation, politely describing such actions as 'undesirable'. As it turned out, the resolution was largely ignored for nearly two decades until Willoughby's hitherto secret world of bribes, insider deals and civic rule-breaking was made public.

The first indications of the scandal that was to engulf Hull's political world emerged in late 1931 when a special committee set up by the Corporation to investigate renewed allegations of suspicious land deals involving councillors sensationally found there was a case to answer. However, the committee's dozen meetings were held behind closed doors and details of the people under investigation were also kept secret, leading to even greater public speculation over who was involved. When the minutes of the committee were finally published in January 1932 they contained no names and made no mention of the fact that several individuals at the centre of the allegations had actually refused to appear before it. The most prominent absentee was one Digby Willoughby.

Thanks to the cloak of anonymity afforded by the decision to hold the committee's deliberations in private, Willoughby could not yet be named

Newspaper cutting from The Daily Mail *on the land scandal — and on Jim Mollison.*

in public even though Hull's chattering classes of the day undoubtedly knew who the finger of suspicion was being pointed at. For his part, Willoughby attempted to counter the rumours over his own actions by claiming he was the victim of a smear campaign aimed at driving him out of public office. His solicitor, James Stickney, would later produce a letter written to the committee on Willoughby's behalf explaining why he had chosen not to attend the hearing. Addressed to the Corporation's Town Clerk, it read: 'I regret I cannot advise my client to attend the inquiry. As you are well aware, there are members of the Corporation who have shown the greatest bias against my client, and it is not proper that he should submit himself to interrogation by these individuals.'

What the minutes did reveal was that 373 separate transactions had been investigated, and in 47 of them members of the council were known to have negotiated on behalf of vendors selling land to the Corporation. The committee's findings were duly reported to a full meeting of the Corporation on 4 February 1932 by Alderman Robert Mell, who had instigated the investigation five months earlier in his role as the then Lord Mayor. One of the committee's recommendations was to submit a request to the Ministry of Health to hold a public inquiry into building and land transactions involving the Corporation during the previous ten years, while Mell moved an amendment to Benno Pearlman's 1915 resolution instructing council officers to take no part in any future contract negotiations involving councillors. Pearlman was more than happy to support the resolution. 'After 17 years the birds are coming home to roost!' he declared triumphantly.

By then an influential Labour figure, it is likely that Pearlman was no admirer of the arch-Tory Willoughby and his contribution to the debate that day left few people in doubt of where he thought the blame for the emerging scandal actually lay.

'During the past few years people in the city have asked me if members of the Corporation are corrupt and if they are above suspicion,' he said. 'My reply on all occasions has been that the Corporation was a body neither corrupt nor under suspicion and I can only express my surprise at the figures given by Alderman Mell. At the same time, I think that the members of the Corporation who have figured in these transactions might be counted on the fingers of one hand.'

Pearlman then reflected on how, despite his original resolution 17 years earlier, not a single council official had ever subsequently drawn his attention to any incidents involving councillors taking a leading role in land deals with the Corporation. 'I think we are entitled to know why the judgement of this council has been flouted by its officials. It has been defied time and time again and no official of this Corporation has had the courage to draw attention to it,' he said. 'There is a reason. Officials are paid servants. There are members of municipal bodies who are very strong personalities and it is not every official, big or little, especially little, who dare take a stand against the big men of the municipalities. This is an explanation to which the public are entitled.'

By this time, Willoughby was no longer a councillor. An election defeat in the city's Newland ward the previous November had ended his lengthy political career. Conscious of the gathering storm and his own failing health, he decided to go on holiday and booked a place on the cruise liner *Laurentic*, completely unaware that a second corruption investigation into his activities was about to come to a dramatic conclusion.

Unknown to Willoughby, the Corporation's special committee continued to look into his business dealings with the authority and unearthed allegations from a firm of tailors that he was demanding and receiving a personal monthly payment of £10 in return for the company keeping its contract to supply clothing to the Corporation. The committee agreed not to take action against the company in return for a full confession over the payments, a move later endorsed by the offices of the Director of Public Prosecutions, which had been alerted to the claims. Safe in the knowledge that no court action would follow, and with his identity kept secret by the committee because of its continued deliberations behind closed doors, a partner with the company revealed how the firm had started supplying clothing for the Corporation shortly after the end of the First World War, obtaining a large contract for police and tramways uniforms. He testified that it was his belief the company had been selected on merit.

The company continued to supply the Corporation with clothing over the next decade but he claimed Willoughby had visited the firm in 1925 shortly before the contract was due to be re-tendered and told the partner and an associate that if they wanted to keep the work they would have to pay him for it. In his evidence to the committee, the partner said he had little option but to agree to Willoughby's demands as the company had recently invested nearly £1,500 in a new manufacturing plant and without the new contract it would struggle to survive. As a result, a deal was struck in which the firm would pay Willoughby £120 a year in monthly instalments of £10, in return for getting the nod on the contract. Payments would be made during the first week of every month by a pre-arranged method which involved the politician telephoning the contractor's shop and setting a time for one of the partners to visit Willoughby's own shop and hand over £10 in notes. Remarkably, these payments carried on in much the same way for the next six years, until the firm's partner, perhaps encouraged by the mounting rumours about suspicious dealings involving councillors in Hull, decided to come forward and reveal what had been going on.

Having considered his statement, the committee decided the matter should be put into the hands of the Chief Constable, and a sting operation was duly mounted by the police with the aim of catching Willoughby red-handed. On the afternoon of 1 March the telephone rang at the tailoring company's shop and a familiar voice announced that he was back from holiday and that 12.30 pm on the following day would be a suitable time for a visit to his shop. Even though he was no longer a councillor, Willoughby was still extracting what amounted to blackmail payments from one of the Corporation's contractors.

The police were duly informed of the proposed rendezvous along with the Director of Public Prosecutions, who had by now sanctioned the investigation under the 1880 Public Bodies' Corrupt Practices Act. Accordingly, when the contractor's son set off for Willoughby's shop on the following afternoon, the numbers of the notes making up Willoughby's usual £10 payment were already known to the police, while officers in plain clothes kept a covert watch on the shop.

As the son emerged from the shop after handing over the money, he was stopped by police officers and taken back into the shop. One of the officers then confronted Willoughby and asked him whether he had received any money from the young man. At first he denied accepting anything and claimed they had simply been talking business. The officer turned to the son and asked him why he had visited the shop. After a moment's hesitation, he told the police what they already knew. 'You hear what he says?' said the officer, turning to Willoughby again. 'Can I give it back?' he replied. Willoughby then led the officers upstairs and into a front room where he pulled away a roll of cloth lying on a counter and picked up a bundle of notes. A subsequent check found the notes were the ones delivered just a few minutes earlier. Asked if he had anything to say after being cautioned, Willoughby replied, 'No, I have no remarks, I must consult my solicitors.' A little over 24 hours later he was dead.

Chapter 4

Hero or Villain?

W<small>E WILL NEVER KNOW</small> whether the priest who helped to conduct the memorial service for Digby Willoughby knew of Willoughby's corrupt dealings over the years he served as one of Hull's leading councillors. Indeed Canon Smallwood's words may well have been spoken in complete innocence. However, they certainly contain a hint of knowledge about what was soon to be revealed in public.

'It is well that the final judgement on us is not that by others but that which is passed on us by God,' he said, before going on to recall some of Willoughby's more respectable achievements while in civic office. 'Now, having served his generation, he has passed on to the other side. There is only One who knows the motives and can weigh up the actions of any one of us. May He who is not only our judge but also our Father, grant both comfort and strength to sorrowing relatives and friends, and to the departed one eternal rest in peace.'

Among the mourners at the service were two men who were to emerge as having played key roles in some of the land-deal transactions exploited by Willoughby. One was political colleague and long-standing friend Alderman Frank Finn and the other was Robert Tarran, one of the city's best-known businessmen. Finn was another well-established figure both at the Guildhall and in the city. He had been a member of the council since 1916, being elevated to the position of Alderman in 1930 in recognition of his service to the authority. Away from politics, his interests included being a director of a timber-importing company and sitting on the board at the popular Tivoli Theatre in the city centre.

During the subsequent Ministry of Health inquiry it was revealed that Finn also profited from Willoughby's dealings over a 15-acre plot of land off Endike Lane. The two politicians had joined forces as partners to buy the land, without Willoughby ever revealing to the original owner that he

was actually the purchaser, instead claiming to be acting as a go-between. As a result, he pocketed £250 per acre as a commission from the landowner for finding interested buyers – who just happened to be himself and Finn. Within a month of the sale, Willoughby was offering the land for sale at an inflated price while purporting to be Finn's agent. This time the purchasers were a syndicate of three local businessmen, one who only knew Willoughby through his public profile on the council, while the others had been friends of Willoughby's for over 10 years. One of these friends was Robert Tarran, probably Hull's best-known pre-war house-builder and developer.

At the inquiry, Tarran would deny having any prior knowledge that the land in question was being earmarked by the Corporation for future house-building, making it potentially valuable in the event of any re-sale. He also denied making any kind of private payment to Willoughby although he acknowledged the deal included a commitment to pay the councillor 25 per cent of the net profit from the future development of the land.

As it transpired, the syndicate simply sat on the land and did nothing with it, waiting for the inevitable approach from the Corporation. The eventual sale to the Corporation went to independent arbitration after the two parties failed to agree on a price. Even so, the three syndicate members finally shared a profit of £1,600 for selling land which had been in their ownership for just a few months

Neither Tarran nor Finn appeared to impress inquiry inspector John Thorpe who, in his final report, singled out both of them for criticism. Finn, he said, appeared to have relied with 'almost childlike faith' on both

Willoughby's judgement and honesty, while Thorpe questioned whether his 'somewhat vague and at times evasive' evidence to the inquiry had actually been truthful. 'The grounds which persuaded Finn to take a small profit must remain in the region of speculation. At any rate they are not, in my opinion, as stated by Finn,' he concluded.

The inspector was equally dismissive of Tarran's repeated denials of suggestions that he had worked secretly in conjunction with the chairman of the housing and planning committee to secure the land, knowing it would eventually be bought by the Corporation.

'As regards Tarran, I was not favourably impressed by the way he gave his evidence,' he concluded. 'Tarran's various references to Willoughby's original participation cannot but encourage speculation as to how they were working together. I am unable to accept Tarran's evidence that he embarked on this transaction after seeing the land and reviewing the position on its merits as a building proposition alone or at all. This statement is not borne out by subsequent indifference to the development of the land. Nor can I accept the explanation in Tarran's case at any rate that Willoughby's participation in the partnership was to reward him for his services in the development of the land. Tarran was fully capable of developing the land had he so desired without assistance from Willoughby. Recalling Tarran's intimate personal relationship with Willoughby, I have come to the conclusion that Tarran's only real interest in the land was to possess and hold it until such time as it should be required by the Corporation. In that future contingency, he would be able to count, if necessary, on the assistance of his friend Willoughby.'

Thorpe also thought it important to highlight the connection between Finn and Tarran, a link not immediately obvious to the casual observer but one which the inspector apparently believed was a key part of the overall picture. It transpired that Tarran regularly bought supplies from Finn's timber company for his own building business and, although ledger accounts for a four-year period revealed the transactions were only a small proportion of his overall timber purchases, Thorpe nevertheless pursued an allegation that Finn had also been promised a share of any eventual development profit on the Endike Lane land by Tarran. True to much of the rest of their evidence given during the inquiry, both men flatly denied that any such arrangement existed and Thorpe, perhaps reluctantly, was unable to unearth any further information on the matter to take it further.

For all the adverse publicity it brought, the Ministry of Health inquiry and Thorpe's resulting damning verdict on him appeared to have little impact on Tarran's reputation or his expanding business empire.

His story was a true rags-to-riches affair. After serving in the Army during the First World War, he started his own one-man joinery business, carrying out building repairs and alterations while operating from a small baker's loft, which he rented for two shillings and sixpence a week. Just over 20 years later his company was employing 10,000 men and women across the country. A skilled engineer, Tarran became the driving force behind a firm at the forefront of modern construction methods. It was said he never ever read a book of fiction in his life, preferring instead to hone his knowledge using the textbooks he studied at Hull Technical College.

After expanding into house-building, he quickly became known for pioneering high-profile local construction projects carried out at almost unheard of speed. Capitalising on Hull's location as a timber port, his joinery works began producing ready-made doors and window-frames for next-day delivery to building sites across the North. Later, he would experiment with building blocks made from compressed sawdust, and pre-cast stone flooring systems using material sourced from gravel-pits in the East Riding. In 1934 his company completed the construction of the Regal cinema in Ferensway in just 17 weeks – six weeks ahead of schedule. Aptly named, the venue was the most luxurious cinema in Hull when it opened and boasted 2,553 seats, including a sweeping single balcony, a 50ft-high screen and a full-length stage. Adding to the building's Art Deco-style glamour, movie star Merle Oberon attended the opening night's screening of Alexander Korda's *The Private Life of Henry VIII* in which she starred with Charles Laughton. The Regal became an entertainment landmark in the city centre for the next 80 years and played host to acts ranging from Laurel and Hardy to The Beatles.

Other Tarran-built landmarks on Ferensway included two imposing office developments, Shell House and Electricity House, and a year after the Regal's opening he accomplished another building feat in Hull that many had thought impossible. Amid increasing concern over the threat to public safety posed by rising traffic levels in the city centre, a review of the existing road network was ordered. Coinciding with moves to fill in the former Queen's Dock to create a new public garden, it presented an opportunity to radically re-design the central area of the city. The main point of conflict between pedestrians and the growing number of vehicles in the area appeared to lie between Whitefriargate, which was then still a through route for traffic, and Queen Victoria Square. In particular, the significant presence of the towering monument to Hull-born MP and famous anti-slavery campaigner William Wilberforce, on the south-eastern edge of the square, was regarded by many as something of an unfortunate physical barrier. The 102ft-high monument's foundation stone had been laid in August 1834, almost a year to the day after the great man's death. A sum of £1,250 was raised from a public subscription to pay for the construction costs and within a few months Hull had a new instantly recognisable landmark that literally loomed over every other building in the town.

A century later Tarran came up with the solution to the congestion in the area and, thanks partly to the fact that he was also a councillor at the time, persuaded the Corporation to back his idea. Typically, he offered the services of his own company to carry out the work and agreed to foot

Robert G. Tarran (top right) with his workmen during the relocation of the William Wilberforce statue in 1935.

the bill in the process. However, this was no ordinary construction project, it was more of a challenge to Hull's great civil engineer of the day. In what he would describe as his own personal gift to the city of Hull, Tarran's bold plan was to move the monument to a new home at the eastern end of the former dock, which was being turned into a public park. In his now trademark style, he also set himself a testing target to complete the work in just three months. True to his word, the monument was carefully taken to pieces and re-built within the scheduled timetable. Some 600 tons of stonework were shifted in the process with less than two per cent of the original structure requiring any repair or replacement. Tarran also added a door to the monument's considerable base platform, allowing access to the hollow interior of the main column for the first time.

His reputation as a philanthropist was enhanced two years later when, along with another local builder, he provided a home to a number of child refugees evacuated from Spain during the country's bloody civil war. Tarran allowed the children to be based in a large house he owned overlooking Pearson Park and became something of a hero to them. When the Second World War erupted and Hull became a target for German bombers, he became a hero to the whole city. In 1940, with the conflict still in its early stages, Tarran encouraged men who worked for his firm to support the war effort by joining the Royal Engineers. Although many of the men were into their thirties and forties, he quickly realised their expertise as skilled engineers and craftsmen would be invaluable and so it proved. They became 694 Company, known as Tarran's Artisan Works, and were whisked off to France almost as soon as they joined up to be given the task of working on the construction of aerodromes. After the allied forces were evacuated from Dunkirk, most of Tarran's men remained in France for another fortnight before finding their way back across the English Channel on a merchant ship sailing out of the French port of St Nazaire. Back in Britain, the company re-formed and set to work constructing sea defences along the East coast from Spurn Head to Scarborough. Their eventful wartime work would later see them join the military campaigns in North Africa and Italy.

Back in Hull, Tarran was spearheading the construction and erection of thousands of air-raid shelters that would subsequently help save countless lives during the relentless bombing of the city. He was also appointed Hull's chief air-raid warden, supervising an organisation of nearly 4,000 volunteer wardens and co-ordinating a series of night-time evacuations into the surrounding countryside. Without the equivalent of London's underground to take refuge in, Tarran identified nearby rural areas where people could escape from the city for the night before returning the next day. Leading by example, he would invariably join the evacuees on their evenings sleeping rough in farmyards and fields. A popular story to emerge at the time was his decision to sleep in a farm's pig sty.

If his name was well-known in Hull, it finally became nationally recognised towards the end of the war when it became associated with the Government's Temporary Housing Programme. Initially announced by Prime Minister Winston Churchill in 1944, the four-year initiative was designed as a response to the acute housing shortage caused by the conflict. Churchill promised 500,000 new homes would be built, most of them bungalows and all of them using non-traditional construction methods in an effort to replace bomb-damaged neighbourhoods. Tarran's track record in adopting new manufacturing techniques and delivering buildings at speed made his company an obvious choice to be one of the 11 firms selected to deliver these new so-called factory homes.

Spurning the use of bricks because they too were in short supply, the homes were simply identified by the name of the company building them. As a result, just over 19,000 Tarrans were completed during the programme, built from pre-cast concrete panels on a wooden frame to a design originally developed in America. They proved to be instantly popular and Tarran, encouraged by their success, developed a larger two-storey version which his firm built in large numbers. Known almost immediately as prefabs, the homes were only supposed to last 15 years as a temporary solution to the nation's housing crisis, but they ultimately proved popular with those who lived in them. In Hull, the Tarran prefabs lasted 50 years, while in other places many still exist today.

At the end of the war Hull faced a massive re-building programme of its own but, instead of playing his customary leading role, Tarran found himself under investigation by Scotland Yard detectives for false accounting. By then, his business empire was crumbling. He had unexpectedly sold his interests in his local companies and announced plans to start a new construction firm in Scotland. Initially, four charges of publishing false balance-sheets were made against Tarran and three other former company officials and these became the subject of a marathon 44-day magistrates' court hearing to decide whether there was a case to answer. Eventually the magistrates decided there was.

The allegations against the man who newspapers would describe as Hull's most 'dynamic and colourful citizen' were eventually aired in December 1947 in a dramatic 32-day trial before a jury in a special assize court held at the Guildhall, the first time such a court had been convened in the city for 150 years.

Along with his co-accused, Tarran faced three counts of publishing false balance-sheets under the Larceny Act of 1861, but by the time the case reached it climax only Tarran and his former company surveyor Herbert Southern remained as defendants, while one of the original charges against them had been dropped. Early in the trial, one of the four defendants - company director Sir Noel Curtis - had been discharged because of a lack of evidence against him. Then, after the closing speech by prosecution barrister Ralph Cleworth, a second defendant was sensationally acquitted. Former company secretary Irvin Haylock walked free from the court after the jury found him not guilty on all three counts on the direction of the judge, Mr Justice Pritchard. Pritchard had actually interrupted Cleworth during his speech to enquire whether he intended asking the jury to find Haylock guilty. Cleworth managed to dodge the question only for the judge to intervene again when he had finished his own address to the jury. 'I think that on the 30th day of the trial, counsel for the prosecution ought to be able to say if he is going to ask the jury to convict Haylock on any of the three counts,' said Judge Pritchard, leaving Cleworth to admit he was not in a position to do so.

Despite Haylock's acquittal, Cleworth was determined to convince the jury they should convict the remaining defendants. He told them: 'It is not my desire to suggest a mean, sordid motive for personal gain against the two accused but I do say that in 1943, if not in 1942, this ship which had carried Tarran to fame in this city and other parts of the country was sinking and if it had sunk the captain and all those in it would have gone as well. I submit you must think that the way it was sought to avoid that wreck was to tide it over until good fortune of some kind would put the company right.'

Cleworth claimed that by publishing false accounts, Tarran had deliberately concealed the company's mounting financial problems from its shareholders. In one example, an actual estimated loss of £232,000 was turned into a £10,000 profit in the company's books, in another a £170,000 estimated loss was reduced to a more palatable £59,000 deficit. The prosecution also alleged that board members at the firm had been deceived on at least one occasion over a Government contract to carry out concreting work at an RAF aerodrome near Pocklington. After the work was carried out, the RAF complained some of it was unsatisfactory and insisted the company should meet 40 per cent of the cost. One of Tarran's directors agreed on the deal but a subsequent board meeting was informed that all remedial work would be paid for by the Government.

Tarran himself claimed to be the innocent victim of a lengthy whispering campaign against him and his company. In a statement made to the police shortly after his arrest, he summed up this view in a few short words: 'It was part of a campaign of bankers to expel me from the great business I have built up for a quarter of a century.' Privately, he told friends he was convinced he was the victim of a plot by local freemasons to discredit him. In reality, the financial chaos caused by the war had eventually been too much for Tarran's company to bear. After deliberating for just over four hours the jury found Tarran guilty of two of the charges and not guilty of a third, while Southern was cleared of all three charges against him. With women openly weeping in the public gallery, the man once at the helm of one Hull's biggest companies was sentenced to nine months' hard labour.

As it turned out, Tarran spent less than a fortnight in the hospital wing of Armley Jail in Leeds before being granted bail pending an appeal against his conviction. The 55-year-old was not deemed well enough to carry out any labouring duties while in prison but appeared to be upbeat on his return to his home in Hull, telling waiting reporters: 'I shall get over this. I want to get back to work and I sincerely hope God will give comfort to those who have stood so loyally by me and that to my enemies He will give forgiveness.' Prominent among those supporters were Hull's coroner, Dr Norman Jennings, and Mrs Barbara Reckitt, the wife of industrialist Arnold Reckitt, who each provided a £500 surety towards his bail.

Tarran's appeal was eventually successful and his conviction quashed but he would never recapture the glory days of his early business career. He died shortly afterwards following a short illness. So was he a hero or a villain? By clearing his name, Tarran managed to preserve his reputation until his death. Those who still remember him or who worked for one of his firms still speak warmly of their old boss. One thing is for certain, there probably won't be another like him.

Chapter 5

The Flying Sweethearts

WHEN THE WHEELS of her Gipsy Moth biplane touched down on Australian soil at the end of an epic 11,000-mile journey on a May afternoon in 1930, a largely unknown young woman from Hull was about to be catapulted to worldwide fame.

In an era when the world of aviation was literally starting to stretch its wings, Amy Johnson's record-breaking solo flight from England to Australia captured the imagination and in the months that followed she received the sort of public acclaim and attention normally reserved for Hollywood's top film stars.

However, while the private lives of the movie industry's biggest names were fiercely protected by an all-powerful studio system adept at manipulating the image of their stars in order to sell cinema tickets, the romance, marriage and subsequent divorce of Amy and fellow flier Jim Mollison were all played out in the full glare of the media spotlight.

Although prone to be boisterous and rebellious, there was little in Amy's childhood to suggest that one day she would become one the best-known women in the world. Born in 1903, her family were immersed in Hull's fishing industry and by the time Amy became a pupil at the Boulevard Secondary School her father was taking over as head of the company which still bears the Johnson name today.

Perhaps the influence of her Danish-born grandfather, Anders Jorgenson, inspired her to dream of a life beyond her home city and he would later play a key role in the build-up to her Australian flight. He had founded the family fish merchants in 1881, taking on British nationality and changing his name to Andrew Johnson as the business prospered. When his eldest son John William Johnson – Amy's father – took over at the helm of the company in 1914, the family was already established as one of the leading members of Hull's fishing community.

With the advantage of enjoying the support of a relatively wealthy family, Amy finished school and took what was then an unusual step for a woman by heading for university. At Sheffield she initially wanted to study to become a teacher but she eventually graduated with a Bachelor of Arts in economics, leaving without completing a fourth year to obtain her teaching diploma.

With still no clear idea about her future career, there was talk about going abroad to work but instead she returned to Hull, briefly working as a shorthand typist for an accountant in Bowlalley Lane before joining a local advertising agency.

Early in 1927 Amy decided to move to London, encouraged by her parents who were not only anxious to see her find a good job but also keen to break up a relationship with a much older Swiss boyfriend whom they disapproved of and who, unknown to Amy, turned out to have been married during their romance. Through a cousin, she started work as a secretary in a solicitor's office but it was to be a Saturday-afternoon bus journey through London which eventually set her on the path to a career in aviation.

Until that moment her only experience of flying had been as a passenger on a five-minute joyride in Hull with her sister some months earlier during a visit to the city by one of the many popular travelling air shows of the era. Contemporary reports suggest she was unimpressed by the flight, but by the time she boarded that bus en route to Stag Lane in Croydon she was intent on joining the London Aeroplane Club and learning to fly herself.

Her arrival at the club must have raised more than a few eyebrows. Despite her family's modest wealth, her background set her apart from the only other women fliers of the era – normally the wives of knights of the realm or rich land-owning aristocrats who had both the time and money to spend on the latest craze. Undaunted by initial scepticism about her natural ability from some of the club's hierarchy, Amy made her first solo flight after less than 16 hours' tuition and eventually gained her pilot's licence after just over a year as a student. By the end of 1929 she had also obtained her ground engineer's licence – the first woman in Britain ever to do so.

Even this feat remained known only to Amy's family and her friends at the flying club, but within a few months her name started to make the headlines after a chance meeting with a newspaper reporter at Stag Lane led to a story about her plans to make a record-breaking long-distance flight. The novelty of epic solo flights had yet to wear off and the public lapped up every new adventure, often reported in vivid detail by competing newspapers eager to land exclusive stories about the latest heroes and heroines of the skies.

In 1928 Lady Heath, Britain's first women's javelin record-holder and something of a daredevil having served as a motorcycle dispatch rider during the First World War, became the first pilot – male or female – to fly solo in a small open-cockpit plane from Cape Town in South Africa to London. She thought it would take her three weeks but the journey actually took three months.

In the following year Lady Bailey, the first woman to fly solo across the Irish Sea, completed a round solo trip between the same two cities, splitting the flights over two periods spanning a total of six months. The daughter of a baron and the wife of a South African millionaire, she started and finish her epic flights at Stag Lane.

Inspired by her fellow female fliers, Amy decided to up the stakes and announced she was planning to become the first woman to fly solo to Australia. It was a bold and brave choice for someone whose longest ever solo flight until that point had been between Croydon and Hull. Without the kind of resources her aristocratic contemporaries could rely on, she embarked on a letter-writing campaign to various public figures in an effort to secure financial support, which met with little immediate success.

In March 1930 two events took place which dramatically changed Amy's fortune. With her hopes of finding a backer seemingly fading, her grandfather Andrew persuaded Amy's father to help by offering to provide up to £800 to buy an aeroplane. At the same time, she wrote to Sir Sefton Brancker, the Director of Civil Aviation at the Air Ministry, after hearing him speak at a lecture hosted by the Royal Aeronautical Society.

In the letter, Amy was brutally honest about her financial circumstances, writing: 'I have for some months been fighting against the lack of enterprise and faith existing in aviation circles. I have a great ambition to do something to help spread interest in aviation in this country, but – I have no money and no influence.'

Despite forgetting to sign her name, Brancker traced Amy to Stag Lane and set up an interview with wealthy businessman Lord Wakefield, a major aviation sponsor and head of the Wakefield-Castrol oil company. The magnate was suitably impressed, offering to share the cost of the plane with the Johnson family and to arrange fuel supplies along the route to Australia. Incredibly, within three weeks of the interview, Amy was setting off from Stag Lane on the journey that would change her life.

Her aim was to beat Australian Bert Hinkler's 16-day record for a solo flight between the two countries, but damage to her plane caused by a crash landing in Burma put her behind schedule. She eventually took 19 days but by becoming the first woman to make the journey alone her place in the history books was guaranteed.

By the time she finally landed in a field in the outskirts of Darwin, newspaper coverage of the flight in both Britain and Australia was occupying most of the front pages. Here was a woman who was not only able to compete with the men but who could also beat them at their own game. Amy's natural good looks were another bonus for the press.

Competition for the exclusive rights to her story had started during the later stages of her flight. The bidding war was eventually won by the national *Daily Mail* in a £2,000 deal partly negotiated through her family. On her arrival in Australia, the *Mail* announced it was paying an additional £10,000 sum in what the paper described as 'the largest amount ever paid to any woman for a feat of daring'. The money was not a gift, but rather payment for Amy's services for the months ahead.

As well as securing Amy's hitherto unknown talents as a regular writer on aviation issues, the deal involved the *Mail* buying her Gipsy Moth aeroplane and arranging a national tour on her return to England as well as having access to her 'exclusive services' – the 1930s equivalent of ensuring that no other newspaper competitor could get close to her.

Less than two days after arriving in Darwin and still exhausted from the journey, Amy was back in her plane for a four-day flight to Brisbane across the arid landscape of northern Australia. Instead of trying to recover from her exploits, a schedule of public appearance had been drawn up by the newspaper and there was no backing out.

As well as the competing media, rival oil companies were also fighting to share some of Amy's new-found fame. Her official escort on the Brisbane flight was Charles Scott, an airline pilot who had been chosen to lead the way because of his knowledge of the route. He was accompanied by a representative from Wakefield-Castrol, Amy's sponsors, but she was also followed by another Gipsy Moth from the Shell oil company.

Scott's barely disguised resentment at being made to act as an air-chauffeur to an unknown woman novice flier was made worse by the presence of the Shell-backed pilot trying to capitalise on the publicity. As a result, he set a ferocious pace in what was a much more powerful machine than Amy's relatively flimsy Gipsy Moth. By the third day of the flight she had given up trying to keep up with Scott and eventually arrived in Brisbane totally disorientated. In front of a crowd of 20,000 waiting to greet her, she ended up over-running the landing strip, striking a boundary fence and crashing her plane, ending upside down in the cockpit. Unstrapping herself, she emerged from the wreckage seemingly unscathed and was even able to deliver a speech of thanks to an official welcoming party. However, after an open-top car parade through the city's streets and yet another official reception, she broke down in a fit of tears.

On doctor's orders, she decided to continue the next leg of her tour to Sydney as a passenger rather than a pilot. A plane was laid on courtesy of Australian National Airways with James Mollison in the co-pilot's seat. The Scottish flier was already an experienced flier and well known as a ladies' man. Whether there was any immediate chemistry between him and Amy is unclear although it is known he managed to get her to promise a dance with him at an evening reception.

As it turned out, Mollison never got his dance with the world's new sweetheart. Instead, her chaperone for the evening, State Governor Air Vice-Marshal Sir Phillip Game, politely told him Amy would not be dancing with anyone because she was extremely tired. Anxious to avoid causing a scene, he took the hint and retired to the bar.

Although they both shared a middle-class upbringing, the contrast between them could not have been greater. Despite her amazing feat, Amy was still regarded as a novice flier with a naïve if enthusiastic approach to life. Mollison, on the other hand, had not only been one of the RAF's youngest officer pilots to see action during the First World War, but had subsequently travelled the world indulging in his twin passions – women and alcohol – with some gusto before joining the newly formed Australian National Airways as a pilot in 1930, flying the firm's primitive airliners carrying passengers and mail across the vast country. Their time together was brief as Amy's tour of Australia saw her move on to Melbourne, Adelaide and Perth. Within a month she left for England and it would be another two years before they met again.

The reception she received on arrival in England was unprecedented. After an enthusiastic welcome at Stag Lane, she was driven with her parents and sisters at walking pace along the 12-mile route to central

London, cheered on by an estimated one million people. Amy and her family were offered the free use of a suite of rooms at the Grosvenor House Hotel in Park Lane while representatives from the *Daily Mail* closely supervised her every move.

The newspaper's planned seven month tour of 40 towns and cities across the country proved to be far too ambitious and arduous for Amy, who was both physically tired and emotionally drained. Her health was a constant concern, prompting a doctor to be on stand-by at the luncheon when the *Mail's* £10,000 sponsorship cheque was presented to her. The tour was abandoned before it really began, although not before Amy arrived back in Hull in August 1930 after receiving a CBE that morning from King George V. If anything, the reception she received in her native city eclipsed the scenes in London, with huge crowds lining the route from Hedon Aerodrome to the Guildhall, where she was the guest of honour at a lavish dinner. At Hedon, the word 'Welcome' had been spelled out on the ground using 1,200ft of calico, ensuring that Amy could see her destination from 15 miles away.

Arrangements had been made for her to come to Hull in another plane but she insisted on using *Jason,* her trusty Gipsy Moth, and on flying alone. Her attachment to the plane would later be tested in a dispute with the *Mail,* who now owned it. With the tour now abandoned, the newspaper wanted to hire another pilot to fly it around the country on promotional appearances but Amy objected and even gave instructions for it to be hidden. The newspaper's owners, Associated Press, eventually relented and gave her *Jason* as a gift, a pay-off for effectively tearing up the £10,000 sponsorship deal.

A final twist came a couple of months later when Amy approached Lord Rothermere, the *Mail's* proprietor, seeking sponsorship for her next record-breaking attempt, a solo flight from London to Peking in China. At the same time she offered to sell *Jason* for £7,300 to the newspaper magnate on condition that the aircraft was presented to the nation. Perhaps mindful of what had happened before, Rothermere declined to offer any sponsorship but did buy the Gipsy Moth, subsequently donating it to the Science Museum in London where it can still be seen today.

Her ill-judged attempt to fly to China got no further than a frozen potato-field in Eastern Europe. She damaged her plane after getting lost en route between Berlin and Warsaw and was forced to give up the flight. Seven months later she was off again, this time accompanied by the London

Aeroplane Club's chief ground engineer Jack Humphreys, heading for Tokyo in a Puss Moth aircraft donated by the de Havilland aviation company. The pair set a new record of ten days but newspapers were full of another new long-distance record – Jim Mollison had reached London after flying solo from Australia in a Puss Moth in less than nine days.

Like Amy before him, Mollison become an instant celebrity, but while she was at times uneasy with the pressures of fame he revelled in the attention and the opportunities it brought, including the same complimentary use of the Grosvenor House Hotel. She sent a telegram of congratulations but they were not to meet again for another seven months. Their paths finally crossed in Cape Town where he had just set another record, flying from London to Cape Town in four days and seventeen hours. She was at the aerodrome to greet him having sailed to South Africa while recovering from an abdominal operation.

It may have been a coincidence for them both to be in Cape Town at the same time, but within two months Mollison had proposed over a lunch in one of London's top restaurants and they married two months after that. The whirlwind romance enthralled the public, not least because Mollison had previously been reported to be engaged to Lady Diana Wellesley, a great grand-daughter of the Duke of Wellington. The day after he proposed to Amy, Mollison took the teenage debutante to the same London restaurant to explain his decision to marry someone else. In view of his behaviour, some viewed the marriage as nothing more than a convenient business arrangement organised by oil magnate Lord Wakefield, who had also sponsored Mollison on his record-breaking flights.

The couple chose to marry in secret without inviting their respective families. Amy deliberately sent her parents a telegram informing them of the wedding just 12 hours before the event in the hope they would not attempt to make the journey from East Yorkshire to London. She made the excuse of wanting a quiet wedding so as not to upset the preparations for Mollison's next record-breaking attempt, a solo flight across the Atlantic. However, her parents and two sisters decided to travel down anyway, only to miss the actual ceremony, arriving unnoticed by Amy just in time to see the happy couple emerging to pose in front of the press cameramen at what they had been led to believe was going to be a low-key event. Amy's disappointed family headed back home without joining the reception at the Grosvenor House Hotel. However, their late arrival at the church was noted in some reports of the wedding.

Amy Johnson with her husband, Jim Mollison, on their wedding day.
Amy Johnson and her husband at Croydon Aerodrome in 1932.

Not for the first time, Amy's motives were being openly questioned. Ever since her bold declaration that she was aiming to fly solo to Australia, some sections of the media appeared to take delight in making thinly veiled attacks on her. Some were no doubt fuelled by prejudice, not only because of her sex but also her Northern roots. In what was still a class-conscious society, Amy was initially dubbed rather dismissively as 'The Flying Typist', and while she consciously tried to hide it, her accent was another source of early amusement among some newspaper critics.

More eyebrows were raised over her attempts to raise sponsorship. Given her background compared to some of her wealthy aristocratic contemporaries, Amy's financial position was never really secure despite apparently lucrative newspaper deals, patronage from wealthy oil magnates and even modelling assignments with top French fashion companies at the height of her fame. Aviation was expensive and the only way to raise money for ever more ambitious record attempts was to seek funding wherever possible. Some critics viewed this as little better than begging and, rightly or wrongly, Amy found herself gaining an unwelcome reputation.

As early as her first tour of Australia, certain sections of the local press Down Under would accuse of her trying to cash in on her new-found fame. One magazine even labelled her as 'The Gimme Gimme Girl'. It was a tag she found hard to shake off. While on honeymoon in Scotland she was reported to have declined an offer to appear on stage at a summer show because there would be no payment, even though the audience had given the couple a standing ovation as well as a spontaneous rendition of *Amy, Wonderful Amy,* a popular song of the time dedicated to the famous flier.

Three weeks after their marriage, Mollison became the first pilot to cross the Atlantic east to west in a light aeroplane in what many still regard as one the greatest solo flights in the history of aviation. On his departure from Portmarnock Sands near Dublin, Amy played the part of the dutiful wife, handing her husband chicken sandwiches, a bag of nuts and raisins, two flasks of coffee and a bottle of brandy to keep him going during the journey. In New York, Mollison was welcomed as a hero and was even given the freedom of the city by the Mayor. Mindful that he was now married, he would later describe his time in Manhattan as 'three weeks of semi-repressed enjoyment'.

Although Mollison's subsequent attempt to achieve a double crossing by completing a west-to-east return leg would be aborted within hours because of bad weather, he returned to England to be greeted with much the same fanfare as witnessed in New York. Together, they were probably the most famous couple in the country and their every move was chronicled by newspapers, newsreel cameras and the first experimental TV crews from the BBC. Mollison was in his element but Amy hated the constant attention. As a result, their marriage was under strain from the very start. Their first serious row came just four weeks after his return to the UK, with Amy storming out of their suite in the Grosvenor House Hotel and briefly returning to her parents' home in East Yorkshire.

Any hopes of the couple spending time together to cement their marriage were also undermined by their quest for new flying records. Amy duly broke her husband's solo record by flying solo to Cape Town, knocking over ten hours off his previous best. After spending three weeks in South Africa, she completed the return journey in another record-breaking time. Once again, the Mollisons were hailed as superstars and on a subsequent holiday in Europe Amy met the famous French designer Coco Chanel, who offered her a choice of any of her evening gowns as a personal gift. Although often uncomfortable in the spotlight, Amy was now not only known for her flying but also for her keen sense of fashion.

After Mollison smashed the record for a solo flight between the UK and South America, the couple teamed up together for an ill-fated attempt on the world long-distance record, which ended in them crashing their twin-engined two-seater biplane 50 miles short of New York. Escaping from the wreckage with non-serious injuries, their dramatic story was once again thrusting them back into the limelight thanks to pre-arranged exclusive newspaper contracts. Another official ticker-tape reception in New York awaited, followed by a Sunday lunch with President Roosevelt and his wife.

Before the attempt, Amy had again attracted some unwelcome headlines over an article under her name in a Sunday newspaper recalling her attempt on the Tokyo record two years earlier. The article had suggested she had been manhandled by a group of peasants after crash landing near Warsaw. The article triggered an investigation by the Polish Aeronautical Club, which not only challenged her version of events but also resulted in a formal complaint to the Royal Aeronautical Club.

Amy was subsequently forced to admit the story had been distorted by the newspaper without her knowledge and she sent a letter of apology to the Polish Aeronautical Club, but it was all too late. The whole story made headlines around the world and she was publicly reprimanded by the Royal Aeronautical Club.

Although Mollison defended his wife, the cracks in their already shaky marriage were starting to appear. Amy's enduring popularity in America would reportedly annoy her husband who, in turn, appeared to be once again living up to his reputation by embarking on a relationship with Princess Arthur of Connaught, the grand-daughter of King Edward VII.

They went their separate ways again at the end of their time together in America, Amy taking up the offer of a short training course with TWA airlines while Mollison headed back to the UK by sea to supervise the construction of a replacement aircraft. When they met again a month later in Toronto, the watching press corps was quick to report that their greeting appeared to be a cool one with no kisses or open displays of affection. Their plan was to continue with the attempt on the world long-distance record by initially crossing the Atlantic back to the UK, but a combination of mechanical problems and poor weather would add to the gathering tensions surrounding the couple. The mood wasn't helped when De Havilland Canada successfully sued them for unpaid garaging and assembly bills relating to their aircraft. Once again they then went their separate ways, Mollison sailing back to the UK with their now dismantled plane, while Amy was admitted to a New York hospital to be treated for a stomach ulcer after she was described as being in a highly nervous condition.

They eventually linked up again in Bermuda for a two-week holiday but it seemed what some described as their second honeymoon failed to spark the necessary magic. Once dubbed 'the flying sweethearts', the reality was now very different and they would spend the next three months apart. Soon after Mollison arrived back in London with Amy still in America, some newspapers started hinting that their marriage was heading for the rocks.

Perhaps conscious of the lucrative nature of their public image, the couple eventually reunited to once again live together in their suite at the Grosvenor House Hotel in London, but it seemed they were practically leading separate lives. They were also spending money freely, Amy on the equivalent of designer-label clothes and fast cars, Mollison on the never-ending social whirl of cocktail bars. Their suite became known as something of an open house while their rows became ever more public.

One on occasion after a violet quarrel, the management was called to clear up blood splattered across the walls of the bathroom. Both were known to have quick tempers and Mollison was often highly aggressive after a drink too many.

Their last flight together was as a team in the 1934 MacRobertson England to Australia International Air Race, which offered £15,000 worth of prizes and a gold cup to the winner, but by the time the competitors gathered for the start of the event the Mollisons were living apart. While her husband remained in London, Amy moved out of the hotel and into a rented cottage in Sussex. She also squeezed in another sailing to America for a business trip and a short holiday. In her absence, Mollison started a romance with actress Dorothy Ward, who was 15 years his senior. Their affair was kept largely secret until his memoirs were published in 1937 when he dedicated the book to her.

Whether Amy knew of the affair while she was away is unclear, but she appeared to shrug off the problems surrounding her marriage by throwing herself into the preparations for the race and the inevitable media attention that came with it. With her husband acting as pilot, Amy once again settled into the role of navigator. One observer at the start of the race seemed to capture the strains between the couple perfectly: 'I saw Jim and Amy climb into their Comet. He looked white as a sheet and as if he had been sloshed for 48 hours which I suspect he was. She looked very nervous and I felt desperately sorry for her having to climb in behind that raffish character for such a venture as this.'

As it turned out, their race started well, with the couple halving the existing record for a flight between England and India by completing the journey in 22 hours. After that, however, things began to go wrong. Problems with a jammed undercarriage, a mix-up over some maps and finally an engine failure put them out of the race before they could clear the Indian sub-continent. An eye-witness where their race finally came to a halt watched as the couple argued loudly with each other over who had been responsible for the engine trouble. A tearful Amy stormed off alone from the aerodrome and found refuge in Allahabad's English Club, where she sent a telegram to Lord Wakefield asking for a loan of £100 to pay for the cost of a flight home by the first airline she could find. After tempers had cooled, Amy had a re-think and the couple decided to travel back home together in their now repaired Comet. Once again, their time together proved to be short-lived as Amy subsequently accepted an offer during a stopover in Cairo to swap places with the engineer sent to repair the plane, who would complete the return journey while she took his far more comfortable seat on an airliner.

Back in England, Amy decided she was not returning to live at the Grosvenor. Instead she accepted an invitation to stay at Dorothy Ward's home, the actress who had secretly been having an affair with her husband. Ward's motives for this offer remain unclear but what is known is that the Mollisons were now a couple in name only. Apart from one joint speaking engagement, they saw little of each other and would set off on separate trips abroad without either being aware of the other's plans. Eventually, Amy moved into the Savoy Hotel while her husband remained at the Grosvenor.

Another short-lived reconciliation ended in yet another row. After Mollison had agreed to live together again at her suite in the Savoy, Amy returned from a theatre trip one night to find him in bed with another woman. Despite his claims they had simply been sleeping off one too many drinks, Amy left the hotel the next morning and went to stay with a friend. In public, they maintained a strained but polite relationship but the writing was on the wall. By the end of 1935 Amy was talking about divorce, but her husband suggested waiting for another six months until he had returned from a planned trip to America and beyond in search of new flying opportunities.

By now, the sceptics who had always viewed their marriage as a convenient business arrangement were probably justified in their opinion. When Amy declared an interest in an attempt to regain her old England to South Africa record, she wrote to her absent husband warning him that no mention of their rift should leak out to the public before the flight. He returned to London two days before her departure, once again promising each other a temporary truce in their barely concealed hostilities until her return.

When she arrived back at Stag Lane after smashing the record for both a single and return solo flight from the Cape, they appeared in public as the happy couple once more. Mollison seemed so carried away by the occasion that he was photographed running alongside her aircraft with his hand on the wing tip as she taxied to a halt.

Back in the headlines, the couple agreed to give their troubled marriage one last throw of the dice. Mollison even admitted his previous extramarital affairs, including one conducted just a month after their wedding.

As they mulled over future possible long-distance flights together, they embarked on a series of public appearances on the back of invitations to social functions across the country, including the official opening of Sewerby Hall near Bridlington, where a crowd of 10,000 turned up to hear Amy's speech. The hall would eventually house a museum dedicated to her memory.

Life on the road together, however, was just as bumpy as in the air. During a visit to Blackpool the couple woke up guests at a prominent hotel in the resort as they argued outside. The row reached a climax when a drunken Mollison fell backwards into an ornamental pond outside the hotel entrance, while Amy jumped into her car and set off for a nearby airport, where she attempted to fly off in their aeroplane. Apparently hysterical, she was persuaded otherwise by the ground crew. A subsequent month-long holiday together on the French Riviera couldn't salvage a lost cause and on her return home Amy instructed her solicitors to start divorce proceedings.

In true celebrity style, Amy announced the impending demise of her marriage to a group of reporters who had been summoned to her home in London. From now on, she told them, she wanted to be known by her maiden name. The following day's editions covered the split in headlines which were soon repeated around the world.

Mollison heard the news in New York where he was preparing to smash another transatlantic record. To add fuel to the fire, he had named his chosen aircraft *The Dorothy* after his lover, the actress Dorothy Ward. When Mollison eventually arrived at Stag Lane after a record-breaking 13 hours and 17 minutes he was asked by one reporter if he would like him to telephone the absent Amy on his behalf. 'Certainly not,' came the abrupt reply.

After their split, Amy checked in at a Swiss clinic to undergo treatment for nervous exhaustion. A recent shoulder injury sustained during a crash landing combined with the strains of her very public matrimonial troubles had left her on the edge of a nervous breakdown. Her estranged husband, on the other hand, embarked on a very public romance with Beryl Markham, another pilot with a racy reputation. One story told how her first husband, furious at her affairs with other men, had angrily banged a row of nails into a post outside their front door to record each one of her encounters in an attempt to shame her.

Always wary of their son-in-law, the Johnson family's worst fears about him were then confirmed when Mollison published an updated version of his 1932 autobiography *Death Cometh Sooner or Later*. The new edition, complete with the apt title *Playboy of the Air* and ghost-written by a *Daily Express* reporter lifted the lid on his marriage to Amy in what today would be regarded as classic kiss-and-tell style. While the Scot was generous to her as a wife and fellow flier, his very public account of his many infidelities were, at the time, seen as both shocking and highly embarrassing to her. To rub salt in the wounds, he dedicated the book to Dorothy Ward.

The couple were finally divorced in August 1938, nearly two years after Amy had initially started divorce proceedings. By then, her fame had started to wane and the luxury lifestyle that came with it was a thing of the past, amid reports of financial hardship and a series of failed romances. The Second World War would provide her with a new mission in life, flying aircraft for the Air Transport Auxiliary, which carried dispatches, mail, medical supplies and personnel across the country. In January 1941 Amy was delivering a plane from Glasgow to Oxford when she crashed into the Thames estuary after getting lost in a snowstorm. Her body was never found.

Even in death, controversy would continue to rage around the girl from Hull. The reasons for the crash remain unclear to this day but the likely explanation is that she was the victim of friendly fire, either from a convoy of warships escorting a number of merchant vessels in the area or from coastal defence batteries.

Chapter 6

The Singer and the Schoolgirl

Tʜᴇʏ ᴀʀᴇ ǫᴜᴇsᴛɪᴏɴs likely to test even most dedicated of pop music historians. Who was the first British male vocalist to earn a gold disc for selling one million copies of the same record? Who was the first British soloist to achieve a Top Ten hit in America's famous Billboard Hot 100 chart? And who was the first British artist to sell one million copies of the same record in America? The answer to all three questions is the same – Hull's David Whitfield.

The career of the former cement-company worker was another classic rags-to-riches story played out in the early 1950s shortly before rock and roll changed the face of pop music forever. His operatic-style tenor voice was a world away from the likes of Elvis Presley yet it still earned him a huge, predominantly female fan base and briefly turned him into an international star. Although his professional singing career never again reached the same dizzy heights of those early years, it would span three decades until his premature death from a brain haemorrhage at the age of 54 while on tour in Australia. By then, however, an almost forgotten sex scandal had seen him effectively turn his back on the UK.

Born in East Street in February 1926, his talent for singing was first developed as an eight-year-old choir boy at St Peter's Church but any thoughts of making a career from his voice were rudely interrupted by the Second World War. At the age of 17, he joined the Royal Navy where he remained for the next seven years, seeing war service as a gunner onboard HMS *Ramillies* during the D-Day landings. The veteran battleship spent a fortnight off the Normandy coast firing a total of 1,002 15-inch shells at German positions in what was thought to have been the greatest bombardment by any single warship at that time.

After the war he served on a number of different vessels from Portsmouth to Singapore and Hong Kong, and started to entertain his colleagues by singing popular songs of the day in impromptu onboard concerts and later as part of full-blown cabaret shows at Navy bases. Shortly before being demobbed in 1950 he was spotted performing in a seaside talent show and was subsequently invited to appear on *Opportunity Knocks,* the radio version of what would become one of the most popular of early TV talent shows. In the programme on Radio Luxembourg and hosted by Hughie Green, he won one round and appeared in an all-winners' show. Further recordings for the show followed, but on returning to Hull he opted for the security of a full-time job rather than chance his arm in the entertainment industry, signing up to load lorries with cement for the Hull Concrete and Stone Company at a local quarry.

On free evenings and weekends the singer took the opportunity to top up his £7-a-week wage by performing in local pubs and clubs, earning between seven and twelve shillings a night depending on the venue and the generosity of its management. His big break came in December 1952 when Hughie Green called to invite him to appear in an after-dinner cabaret show in London. Among those at the show was impresario Cecil Landeau, who was credited with discovering Audrey Hepburn. Landeau was there to see a dancing act but was so impressed by Whitfield that he offered the singer a contract to appear at Mayfair's Washington Hotel. Also in the audience was a talent spotter from the Decca record company. Within 24 hours Whitfield was in a Decca studio recording a test session. The label was also impressed and in January his debut record *Marta* was released. For a relative unknown, 20,000 sales in just four weeks were enough to convince Decca executives that a potentially profitable star was in the making. A second record was cut featuring the song *I Believe.* However it failed to make an impact because a rival version by the already-established American singer Frankie Laine stormed to the top of the charts and stayed there for an incredible 18 weeks.

The chart rivalry between the two singers intensified later that year when they again released the same song at the same time. Starting life as a German song called *Mutterlein, Answer Me* holds a unique claim to fame by being the only song to knock itself off the top of the UK singles chart. It also saw Laine's initial version being banned by the BBC for its opening line 'Answer me, Lord above', as censors at the Corporation deemed it to be an attempt at mockery of Christian prayer. Whitfield's quick-witted producer Bunny Lewis spotted an opportunity and changed the line to 'Answer me, oh my love.' With airplay now guaranteed it did the trick and hit the Number One spot on November 7, only to be knocked off by Laine's version a week later despite the BBC ban.

Whitfield's rising popularity triggered a regular production line of successful singles until Lewis and his orchestral arranger Mantovani came up with the song that ensured his place in chart history. They wrote *Cara Mia* under two pseudonyms but there was no hiding place from the song itself as it went to the top of the British charts and stayed there for ten consecutive weeks. It was also a hit in America and went on to sell over three million copies around the world, eventually providing the name for a string of his own cars and a luxury house in Kirk Ella. Suddenly, the former sailor from Hull was a household name.

Today's generation may wonder what all the fuss was about, but in 1954 the age of celebrity was only just dawning and popular music, albeit still waiting for the excitement of rock and roll, was at the forefront of it all. Although married with a young son, Whitfield was still young enough at the age of 28 to instantly attract an army of mostly female fans. The nickname he gave to his most fanatical female followers was 'bobbysoxers', a description first given to Frank Sinatra's teenage fans a decade earlier. While fame brought adulation, money and several high-profile trips to America, its darker side quickly became an unwanted feature in his life. In a remarkably candid self-penned article in the *Hull Daily Mail* in November 1954 he hit

David Whitfield posing with his new Jaguar complete with personalised number plates.

out angrily at rumours surrounding his private life and aimed a hefty swipe at some of the inhabitants of his home town in particular. 'Since I have become a singer, I have learned a lot. Every day my education is continued,' he wrote. 'The round of theatres, personal appearance and other engagements that the top-liner faces six days out of the seven – on the seventh he travels – is a school in which you learn how crazy people are.'

While bobbysoxers attempting to climb through his dressing-room window, jumping on his moving car and grasping for any memento they could lay their hands on were gently chided for being crazy but essentially nice kids, he went on to describe 'a more dangerous problem that everyone faces when his name goes up in lights. That problem is made by the rumour-mongers. Perhaps it's not surprising that the bar-flies whose poisonous speciality is slanging me are entirely confined to Hull. Not surprising – but very distressing for I'd accept one Hull in exchange for three Bahamas any day. Still, there they are. Just kick aside any stone and you can find them crawling hurriedly to another dark hole. They say that Sheila (his wife) and I have broken up. They say we are having a divorce. They say that my son, Lance, is nearly dying. They say I have developed a greater affection for the bottle than for singing. And they say that I am being soaked again if I dare to take any relatives for a quiet drink in Hull. That particular smear is bad enough to make it taboo for me to buy a round of drinks when I am with some relatives, particularly my father-in-law.'

For someone supposedly enjoying the fame and fortune he had worked so hard for, it was bitter stuff. He went on: 'I suppose these rumours will always fly when the procession of so-called friends, spivs, waiters and hangers-on see the apparently gay social and business treadmill of the star. Of course there are temptations enough to lead astray a dozen Adams. Those who know me realise that I enjoy the fun and dodge the temptations. It isn't that I am in the running for a halo but any sensible chap in my place would realise that if he accepted every drink offered him he would live in a shady land of perpetual hangovers which isn't fun. He would realise that one ambiguous or compromising scheme in the dressing room couldn't be wiped out by a century of penance. That's why I leave my dressing room wide open when a particularly insistent fan comes in to see me and why I'm never alone when there are bobbysoxers in the vicinity.'

Despite his misgivings about the trappings of fame, the Whitfield publicity machine in the capable hands of his manager Reg Warburton showed no signs of spluttering to a halt. More hit records and sell-out tours followed and there was even a trip to America for a Hollywood screen test. Nothing ever came of it but the accompanying stories and Whitfield's easy affability with reporters ensured he was rarely out of the show-business columns of the newspapers. When he was finally presented with his Gold Disc for selling a million copies of *Cara Mia,* 1,000 members of the David Whitfield Fan Club packed into Blackpool's Winter Gardens for the club's first-ever convention to witness the occasion. To match the seaside surroundings, fans were given sticks of rock with the singer's name running through them.

For a while, the global success of *Cara Mia* made Whitfield the most popular young singer in Britain. However, his traditional background in the pubs, clubs and cabaret bars together with his operatic musical style meant he was more at home in the comfortable arena of light entertainment as a balladeer than the new, emerging, unpredictable world of rock and roll, where the likes of Bill Hayley and Elvis Presley and, closer to home, Cliff Richard, would change the look and sound of the charts forever. Diversions into theatre tours starring in the musical comedy *Rose Marie* and a number of pantomimes only served to underline his broader appeal to an older audience.

While his time at the top of the charts was limited to just a few years, that appeal still guaranteed a sizeable following and resulting attention wherever he performed. However, his earlier misgivings about fame came back to haunt him in 1966 when two separate court cases nearly derailed his career completely. The first was played out before a jury at a court in Chesterfield, when a salesman called George Coyle appeared to plead not guilty to a charge of assaulting the singer and causing him actual bodily harm. By the time the case reached court, fans of Whitfield had already been given a preview of what to expect by the man himself. Never shy in coming forward and speaking to the media, he had given an interview shortly after the incident in a cabaret club in Chesterfield detailing how he had been punched in the eye by an irate member of the audience apparently upset by the attention he was giving to the man's wife during a rendition of *A Spoonful of Sugar* from the hit musical *Mary Poppins.* The man had grabbed him by the hair and hit him in the face.

'I just can't drop the matter, my looks have been quite badly damaged,' he told the *Hull Daily Mail,* referring to plans to see a solicitor about the assault. Nursing a black eye and five stitches but apparently happy to pose for photographs, he went on: 'I was so shocked at first, I just carried

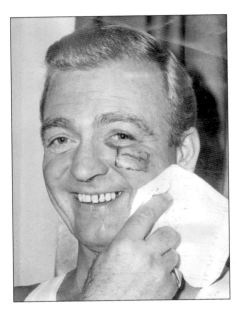

David Whitfield, shows off his black eye after the nightclub attack in Chesterfield.

on singing. Not until I noticed my shirt and jacket soaked in blood did I realise what had happened. Had I realised what damage he had done I would probably have given him one back. Earlier in the same evening I picked out the same girl to dance with me as I sang *I Kiss Your Hand Madame*. I kissed her and led her back to her table where she was sitting with about a dozen other people. This sort of thing is a routine part of my act, a personal touch which the girls generally love. This one was about 20. I thought she was single and she seemed to enjoy my singing. This sort of thing could have happened anywhere. It is all part of show business. I suppose I found the whole thing rather amusing but I can't let this man get away with what he did.'

The *Mail's* interview also carried a quote from the cabaret club's manager, Rosendo Cervello, who appeared to side with the singer. 'The way David carried on with his act was wonderful and he got tremendous applause. The man who hit him was the girl's husband. I have barred him from the club but I cannot disclose his name. I will give the name to David later if he wants to take action,' he said.

Just over two months later the man in question, George Coyle, was in court facing an assault charge with David Whitfield as the main prosecution witness. Giving evidence, he said the incident came after an otherwise uneventful week of shows at the cabaret club during which he always carried out the same routine of choosing a female member of the audience to perform a song and dance routine to *I Kiss Your Hand Madame*. On each occasion, he said, he kissed his dancing partner on the hand.

The singer told the court he asked permission to dance with Mrs Coyle and, although she appeared to be very nervous, she had not raised any

'I kiss pretty girls with more pleasure',

—ADMITS DAVID WHITFIELD

9 MAR 1966

SINGING STAR DAVID WHITFIELD told a jury at Derbyshire Q... that during his stage act he did not always choose pretty girls ... admitted that he kissed them with more pleasure.

"I kiss ladies on the lips because ... pleasure out of it and so does the ... ...," he said under cross-exa...

Appleby defends...
...ken Coyle, a 30-year-...
..., of Shelford-road,
...ttinghamshire, who...
... of assaulting Mr
...sing him actual...
... He pleads not...

... out of an...
...erfiedi's Carl...
...where it is...
...£14 a week...
...r Whitfield...
... had kisse...
...6-year-o...
...yle. ...

'Whitfield kisses upset me'

—SAYS WIFE

1 8 MAR 1966

A 30-YEAR-OLD HUSBAND accused of assaulting singer David Whitfield and causing him
bodily harm at a Chesterfield night club was found
not guilty.

Mr Whitfield, of Cara Mia, Kirkella, had described as
Derbyshire Quarter Sessions how he was struck in the face
by the husband of a woman he had kissed and danced with as ...
part of his set at Chesterfield's Carlton Cabaret Club ...

But the woman told the court ...
...her and made her shake with ... ...ably as nervous as any woman...
...embarrassment of ... ...would have been under the
Accused was George M... ...circumstances, said Mr Dineen...
Whitfield, £14-a-week salesman, of ... Mr Whitfield said when ...
Coyle, Shelford-road, Gedling, Notts ...things u I'll Kiss you' Little
He pleaded not guilty. ...sing he placed his finger on ...
Mr rem Dineen, prosecuting ...Lips" cheeks and kissed her on ...
said that Mr Whitfield who ...her while singing.
believed in 'audience partici- ...Spoonful of Sugar, he went...
pation,' walked around ...over he was about 2ft, away...
audience and chose Coyle's ...her, Mrs Coyle and sang and ...
wife to dance with him. ...from her when he was seized
...by the hair and struck in...
... said ...the face by Coyle. He had ...
...on to dance ...five stitches put in the woun...
...m and, although ...oth...
...very nervous. she
objection.
They danced toge...
...subdued lighting ar...
...her hand and 'pec...
...the lips.
Whitfield said M...
a "sport" to get...
was no sinister...
approaching her...
"I thought I'd...
up a little bi...
nervous."
Asked how h...
nervous, Mr ...
"Because som...

NO OBJECTION

Autograph hunter accuses David Whitfield

HULL - BORN singing
... star David Whitfield
...recently exposed him-
self to one of four young
autograph - hunting girls
who went to the bunga-
low where he was stay-
ing, it was alleged at
Llanrwst Magistrates
Court, Denbighshire, to-
day.

1 0 OCT 1966

Later, said Mr John Lloyd
Morgan, prosecuting, he committed an offence against the
girl, aged 11, and asked her to
return next day alone.

Whitfield, 40-year-old star of
the "Gaytime" summer show
at Llandudno, denied charges
of indecent exposure and
indecent assault.

65

objection. He admitted kissing her on the hand and then giving her a 'peck' on the lips, insisting there was nothing sinister in his actions. 'I thought I would try to cheer her up a little bit as she was nervous,' he said. Asked by prosecutor Tom Dineen how he knew she was nervous, he replied, 'Because some ladies put their arms around me and squeeze me and say they have been waiting for this for a long time.'

Cross-examining, the defence counsel Brain Appleby wasted no time in painting a very different picture. He claimed Whitfield had pulled Mrs Coyle onto the dance floor without asking for permission and had kissed her with an unwarranted degree of intensity. Asked if he thought it was his privilege to kiss girls, Whitfield probably came to regret the answer he gave. 'In certain cases, yes. I kiss ladies on the lips because it's in the song. I get pleasure out of it and so does the audience and sometimes the girl,' he replied.

Club manager Rosendo Cervello and an off-duty special constable who was in the audience on the night in question both told the court there seemed to be nothing improper in the singer's act, but Coyle and his wife Barbara had other ideas. Giving his own evidence, the defendant said Whitfield had forcibly pulled his wife onto the floor: 'He nearly pulled her off her feet. It was quite sudden and he didn't ask permission. He got hold of her very closely. My wife kept looking at me appealingly. He kissed her quite roughly on the mouth. It was very forcible and I thought it was indecent. I couldn't believe it. She looked frightened and upset.' Coyle claimed he asked Whitfield if he would mind leaving her alone and the crooner went away from their table only to return later on while singing *A Spoonful of Sugar*. 'He started singing and she turned her face away. He crouched or knelt down and brought his face level with my wife. I got the impression he was going to kiss her again so I took hold of his hair and pushed him away with the flat of my hand. I was absolutely desperate. My wife looked so frightened. I really felt embarrassed for her. What else could I have done?' Asked about the cut on the singer's face, Coyle said he didn't know whether it was caused by his hand or Whitfield's microphone.

In her own evidence, Barbara Coyle stuck by her husband's version of events. She claimed she had been pulled from her seat without giving her consent and was twice kissed 'intimately' on the lips. She told the court she was unable to move because the singer was holding her head. 'I was shaking with embarrassment and was very upset,' she continued, describing how with the second kiss he had jerked her chin around very sharply with his hand. 'He said, "This is where I am, not over there." I did not encourage him. I did not enjoy my meeting with David Whitfield.'

The jury sided with the couple and Coyle was found not guilty. While not hugely damaging, the case fuelled more speculation about the singer's behaviour. His own evidence in court that being attractive to woman was effectively part of his job description as a singer of largely sentimental ballads only served to fuel long-standing rumours about his private life. With an easy charm and a willingness to play up to the attention given to him by some of his female fans, he had plenty of admirers. Yet he also made great play of being a family man, happily posing for the cameras with his wife and young children whenever the opportunity arose. Despite Whitfield's attempts to make light of the case – describing the whole affair as 'comical' – he would be back in court seven months later. This time he was the defendant and the charges were much more serious.

When he appeared at Llanrwst Magistrates' Court in north Wales in October 1966, his career had arguably reached its lowest point. His deal with Decca had long since come to an end, chart appearances were firmly a thing of the past, and bouts of heavy drinking were an open secret in show-business circles without ever being reported in the newspapers. The incident in Chesterfield had ultimately proved an embarrassment but it didn't stop him securing a starring role in a summer variety show in the seaside town of Llandudno. True, it was a far cry from the days when he was a regular at the London Palladium but it was still work. During the show's run he stayed in a rented bungalow in the nearby village of Glan Conway and it was here that four young girls called one day to ask for autographed photographs of the 40-year-old singer.

The girls – one aged eight and the others eleven – went to the kitchen door, where they were greeted by Whitfield. He told them he couldn't give them any photographs because he was busy talking to his manager. Instead he asked them to call back again later in the day. The girls duly returned in the late afternoon and again knocked on the kitchen door. The singer once again opened the door and this time agreed to give the girls some photographs which were kept in his car on the driveway. Wearing just a shirt and short trousers, he sat in the car with one leg on the driver's seat and the other outside the car as he signed the photos while the girls queued up for their turn.

It was at this point that one of the 11-year-olds would later claim that Whitfield exposed himself to her. The prosecution's case, outlined by Mr

Lloyd Morgan, then alleged the group returned to the kitchen having received their photographs, only for the singer to suggest they might also each like a stick of his personalised rock – the same type of rock handed out at his fan club's first annual convention in Blackpool just over a decade earlier. Mr Morgan told the court it would be alleged that, while they again returned to his car to collect the rock, the singer told the girls to go back to the bungalow but asked the same 11-year-old girl to stay with him.

He went on: 'As this girl was looking down into the boot of the car, Whitfield put his hand down the front of her dress. She pushed him away and Whitfield told her, "I won't do anything to hurt you." ' The pair then returned to the bungalow where Whitfield told the girls it was time to go. However, Mr Morgan then claimed he asked the same girl to stay behind, before asking if she would like to come to tea by herself the following day. She replied she would only do so if she could bring her younger sister with her. Mr Morgan then claimed Whitfield asked the girl not to tell anyone about it and made her promise several times before allowing her to catch up with the others. On their way home, continued Mr Morgan, the girl started to cry because, as a Girl Guide, she had made a promise and had a duty to stick by it even though she knew it would be wrong to go back the next day. When the girl's aunt later discovered her crying and distressed, she broke down and told her everything.

The aunt contacted the police and the girl gave a statement. Describing the incident at the car, she said: 'He asked me to put my hand on his knee but I quickly took it off again. He gave me three sticks of rock. As I was looking down into the boot he put his arm round me and tried to put his hand down my dress. I pushed him away. Later he asked me to stay alone and to go by myself the next day. I had no intention of going because I did not like him. He told me not to tell anyone and made me promise about five or six times.'

Whitfield was interviewed by police the next day at the bungalow. Asked if he had exposed himself, he replied, 'God strike me down. I did not do such a thing. It makes me sick.' When asked if he had placed his hand down the girl's dress, he said, 'Where do they get all this from? I did not touch her at all.' When the detective sergeant conducting the interview told him that the girl seemed a sensible type and that, as a Girl Guide, she had been very upset at the prospect of having to break her promise not to tell anyone, the singer replied, 'Oh, is she indeed?' Read out in court, his replies to the police did him few favours. When the detective had asked what he thought about the girls' behaviour, he said, 'I thought they were cheeky buggers.'

The only witness called by the defence was not Whitfield but an accounts clerk called Marjorie Woodcock, teasingly described in newspaper reports of the case as 'an attractive blonde'. Originally from Bury in Lancashire, she told the court she had known the singer for around eight years and was staying at the bungalow when the children called. She confirmed she was in the bedroom at the time and had listened to the conversations between the singer and the girls, recalling the chat had lasted for about five minutes. She said she heard nothing out of the ordinary being said between them. Cross-examined, Miss Woodcock acknowledged she had not actually seen what had happened because she had been asked to keep out of sight 'for obvious reasons'. Lloyd Jones, Whitfield's counsel, later paid tribute to her 'great courage' for giving evidence in what were potentially embarrassing circumstances.

'Is it likely,' he asked the court 'that this man would choose to behave indecently with little girls when his girlfriend is a few yards away to hear any outcry or complaint? You see that she is not an unattractive lady. So is it likely that he would indulge himself with these children? We have a man of 40 who is married and has a wife with three children. He and Miss Woodcock were staying together in this bungalow. That may not be a very creditable thing to do but this not a court of morals.'

Jones' defence strategy of calling Woodcock as his main witness meant Whitfield's affair with her was exposed and it ensured he made an unwanted return to the headlines of the national newspapers. It was also somewhat inevitable as she had been interviewed by the police at the time. One way or another, her presence at the bungalow would have been revealed.

After a five-hour hearing the singer was found guilty on the charge of indecent exposure and was fined the maximum of £25 and ordered to pay £25 costs. He was acquitted on the other charge of indecently assaulting the same girl by putting his hand down the front of her dress. His carefully cultivated image of a family man was shattered as the case revived memories of the womanising rumours he so angrily dismissed when he first became a household name, yet his marriage to Sheila would survive the scandal. However, his singing career, particularly in the UK, never fully recovered, and bookings dried up to such an extent that he increasingly turned to Canada and Australia for regular work and touring.

Chapter 7

Fish, Ships and Spies

Bill Rodgers, or Baron Rodgers of Quarry Bank to give him his official title, cemented his place in British political history when he left the Labour Party to help form the Social Democratic Party. The divisive move came two years after Margaret Thatcher's dramatic triumph in the 1979 General Election at a time when Labour was drifting leftwards under the leadership of Michael Foot. Joining former Labour cabinet colleagues Shirley Williams, David Owen and Roy Jenkins in the breakaway SDP, he was perhaps the least known member of the quartet despite having served in Labour governments under both Harold Wilson and Jim Callaghan. His subsequent autobiography was titled *Fourth Among Equals,* ironically reflecting his low-profile membership of the so-called 'Gang of Four'.

His role in Hull's history of scandals is more obscure yet he inadvertently ended up playing a pivotal part in one of the most heated and enduring controversies the city has ever witnessed. In August 1974 Rodgers was Labour's Defence Secretary. It was a time when Cold War tensions between the Soviet-dominated Eastern bloc and the United States and her Western European allies were still capable of making headlines. Add to the mix the hostilities between the UK and Iceland over disputed fishing rights in the so-called Cod Wars and it was clear that he certainly had a big job on his hands. Against this turbulent background, the disappearance of a Hull trawler in heavy seas off the coast of Norway not only found its way into the national media spotlight but triggered a remarkable cover-up perpetuated by successive governments over the following three decades.

The human price paid by Hull's fishing community down the years was nothing new. Catching deep-water fish was, and still is, regarded as one of the most dangerous jobs in the world. Grief and loss were features of everyday life for families with men at sea, none more so than in early 1968 when three trawlers from Hull were lost within days of each other. What became known as the Triple Trawler Tragedy was the worst UK fishing industry disaster of the 20th century. The *St Romanus, Kingston Peridot* and *Ross Cleveland* went down in vicious storms off the coast of Iceland with the loss of 58 men. Almost exactly six years later, the *Gaul* was added to the long list of trawlers destined never to return to the Humber estuary and the safety of St Andrew's Dock.

For years, most trawler losses were grudgingly accepted by the city's fishing community as an inevitable part of going to sea. However, the tragic events of early 1968 changed all that when a group of fishermen's wives and family members famously led by Lil Biloca launched a campaign to improve safety onboard the vessels. The women secured meetings with trawlers owners, local MPs and then took their case to government ministers in London, all played out in front of TV cameras and newspaper photographers. Although not immediately apparent at the time, the media coverage of the campaign created a momentum all of its own. For the first time in over a century, the industry's key figures were being called to account in a very public fashion and politicians were being put under direct pressure to act or at least be seen to be doing something. The trawler owners were immediately instructed to implement new safety measures, while subsequent official inquiries into the sinking of each trawler led to tighter regulations covering design and construction, the provision of additional safety equipment onboard, new legal standards for radio equipment operators and an overhaul of employment, training and working practices.

Six years later, the seemingly baffling disappearance of the *Gaul* in similar weather conditions to those experienced by the doomed Triple Trawler crews would trigger an even greater public outcry. Significantly, it was also fuelled by relentless media coverage, some of which would only serve to cloud the issue. From the famous ghost ship *Flying Dutchman* to the still unsolved puzzle of the crewless *Marie Celeste,* maritime history is littered with stories of unexplained mysteries. Most belong to the days when tales from the oceans were passed between crews and through the ports they sailed from. As such they would invariably change with every telling, facts being replaced by colourful invention and fantasy along the way. Although the *Gaul* sailed in a very different era of hi-tech navigational aids, the story of her disappearance also became the stuff of folklore and legend. The apparent absence of any confirmed location for the wreck on

the bed of the Barents Sea where she had been fishing only served to heighten speculation about her fate.

For nearly a quarter of a century debate raged over what had happened to the trawler. Much of it was speculative and based on conspiracy theories. The official conclusion of a formal public inquiry held later the same year pointed to the *Gaul* being swamped by a succession of huge waves striking with such deadly speed and force that the crew did not even have time to issue a distress call. After the wreck was finally located in 1997, the official inquiry into her loss was re-opened and subsequently answered many of the questions raised by the crew's relatives during the intervening years. While the inquiry patiently debunked the many conspiracy theories it also laid bare a Cold War cover-up which had been officially denied for decades.

The *Gaul* started life as the *Ranger Castor,* the fourth and final vessel in the *Ranger C* class. Built by Brooke Marine in Lowestoft, the stern trawler was launched in December 1971 and completed her maiden voyage in the following October. The *Rangers* were the latest generation of factory fillet freezer trawlers, distinct from whole freezer trawlers which were crewed solely by fishermen who would carry out the job of hauling, shooting and maintaining the fishing gear as well as gutting and storing the fish. In contrast, fillet freezers would carry a number of factory-hands who took no part in the actual fishing. Working on a separate factory deck, their job consisted of filleting and packing the fish before freezing it and then stowing it away in the hold. Boasting far superior crew accommodation than their smaller, older counterparts, such was the perceived luxury of the new freezer vessels that some even dubbed them 'Floating Hiltons' after the upmarket international hotel chain.

A change of ownership in mid-1973 saw a name change for all four trawlers, and the re-christened *Gaul* completed her fourth fishing trip shortly before Christmas that year. On 22 January 1974 she set sail from Hull for what would be the last time. Onboard at the time was her regular mate George Petty, but during the voyage he was injured in an accident and was replaced by Maurice Spurgeon. Such crew substitutions were common but few inadvertently saved one life while sealing the fate of another.

The last message sent from the *Gaul* was a private telegram sent at about 11am on 8 February. At the time she was believed to be some 80 miles north of North Cape off the coast of Norway. Although the weather was bad in the area other similar fishing vessels rode out the storm, including two of her sister trawlers. The first indication that something was wrong came later that afternoon when the *Gaul* failed to submit a scheduled report on her position and fishing schedule. A subsequent search operation was mounted by the Norwegian authorities in conjunction with the RAF and the Royal Navy. For four days an area of 117,000 square miles was covered, with 23 trawlers joining in the search, but no trace of any wreckage was found. A week later an RAF Nimrod carried out another sea search again without any success and while shipping and aircraft in the area were asked to maintain a look-out for signs of the *Gaul* over the following weeks nothing was spotted.

Nearly three months later, on the morning of 8 May, the first evidence from the *Gaul* was found in the shape of a lifebuoy. Marked with the words *Gaul Hull,* it was discovered by a Norwegian skipper some 80 miles from the last known position of the trawler. Until the wreck was finally located in 1997, the lifebuoy remained the only physical reminder of the missing vessel and, as such, became the focus of several of the more colourful conspiracy theories surrounding the saga. By the time the lifebuoy was displayed at the formal inquiry which got underway in September that year some relatives were convinced the *Gaul* had been engaged on a spying mission. Until then, there had never been any official acknowledgement that British trawlers had ever been used by the Royal

Navy to carry out covert observations on the rival Russian fleet. Even so, it wasn't much of secret to many in the local fishing industry and word soon spread to the city's MPs.

In July 1974 John Prescott, then a relatively new MP, wrote to the Ministry of Defence asking for details about naval personnel sailing on British trawlers, enclosing a letter from a manager with the Hull firm Hellyer Brothers, referring to an example of an officer being taken on a fishing trip on a Hellyer trawler. The reply from Frank Judd, the Parliamentary Under Secretary of State for Defence, spelled out the ministry's position: 'I can confirm that Royal Navy personnel do embark on trawlers from time to time. In addition to the example referred to, it is by no means unusual for junior officers to spend some time on board trawlers to gain sea-going experience. There is nothing strange about this, given the close relations between the Royal Navy and the fishing fleets in both peace and war. I can, however, appreciate how distressed the relatives of the crew of the *Gaul* must be and I would be grateful, therefore, if you could assure them that the occasional presence of RN personnel in trawlers need give no cause for concern. I should also like to make it clear that there were none on the *Gaul*.'

Judd's reply was picked up by several newspapers who quoted an angry Prescott. 'The Russians use trawlers to gain military secrets and I want to find out if this means we are doing the same,' he was quoted as saying. 'If the Russians arrested a trawler and discovered a Royal Navy man onboard, it could put the crew in an extremely difficult and perilous situation. Would the world really believe that the Royal Navy man was simply aboard to gain sea-going experience?'

The Hull North MP Kevin McNamara also waded into the debate. 'We want to know whether the Navy men are dressed in civilian clothes, whether the crews know they are aboard and whether the crew have any choice about whether they sail or not with Navy personnel. It seems that the crews have been completely unaware of this happening,' he said. *The Daily Mail* also spoke to Tom Boyd, head of the Hull-based trawler firm Boyd Line. 'My firm has not carried a Navy man for about six years,' he said. 'When we did carry them, they were obviously bound for the Royal Navy Fishery Protection Service and it was decided that they should see how our boys worked.'

With the story showing no signs of going away, Defence Minister Bill Rodgers then entered the fray in a letter sent to Hull's three MPs. It confirmed what he had personally told them a few days earlier after being briefed by senior ministry officials. He wrote:

'First, may I say how completely I understand and appreciate the fears and the anxieties of those who lost members of their family on the *Gaul*. However, I can categorically assure you that no RN personnel or MoD equipment were onboard the *Gaul*. I can also assure you that the British trawler fleet is not involved in any way in intelligence gathering: this applies as much to equipment as to personnel. As you know, the Royal Navy runs a scheme by which Naval officers gain experience of the day-to-day work of the fishing fleet (and the Merchant Navy as a whole). This of course contributes to good relations between the two services. Ten junior Naval officers in all have gone to sea in trawlers under this scheme in the last five years and about 30 in all have used other merchant ships over the same period. There may well have been other occasions outside the formal scheme when Royal Navy officers have gone to sea in fishing and other merchant ships. We would not necessarily have kept a record of each occasion. They go onboard to get general experience or, in the case of trawlers, to find out what fishery protection is all about by familiarising themselves with the problems of fishermen. They do not of course displace regular members of the crew by, for example, acting as radio operators.

'Apart from such sea-going experience, there have only been two other occasions in recent times on which MoD personnel have been embarked on trawlers. These were when Royal Navy officers from the Hydrographical Service (one on each occasion) took part in an exercise to check the radio navigation chain by reference to the satellite navigation system in the area where the trawler was due to fish. The opportunity was also taken to try to find some equipment which had been lost. Up to now we had believed that the presence of naval officers from time to time was well known to the trawler men of Hull and that they were happy with the arrangement.'

Over 20 years later, when interviewed following the discovery of the *Gaul* by a team led by freelance journalist Norman Fenton, Lord Rodgers admitted that as Defence Minister he had been misled by his officials when briefed on the extent of Royal Navy activity onboard trawlers. As Mr Justice David Steel subsequently noted in the final report of the re-opened formal investigation into the loss of the *Gaul*: 'Since many of those connected with fishing in Hull were aware that at least the second paragraph of the (Rodgers) letter was economical with the truth, it was inevitable that there was extreme scepticism about these assurances. This most unfortunate state of affairs then festered for nearly quarter of a century.'

Local suspicion over a Russian connection to the mystery of the *Gaul* was understandable if totally misplaced. Some pointed to the history books and the so-called Russian Outrage of 1904, when a number of Hull trawlers were attacked by the Russian Navy after being mistaken for enemy Japanese boats. One trawler was sunk and two Hull fishermen died, while the embarrassed Russians eventually paid £66,000 in compensation. If it could happen once, some believed it could happen again. Others favoured a more sinister Cold War explanation, suggesting the crew had somehow been captured and taken prisoner. One relative even wrote to Prime Minister Harold Wilson claiming two Royal Navy officers had not only been onboard the *Gaul* at the time but were also the reason why two Russian gunboats had escorted her from the fishing grounds to an unnamed Russian port. Those who believed the Russians had seized the *Gaul* and were holding the crew against their will tended to overlook the obvious impracticalities of carrying out such a feat in what were very bad weather conditions or the fact that no diplomatic game of chess followed. There was certainly no sign of any of a captured crew being paraded in front of the cameras by the Russian military, eager to indulge in a spot of Cold War one-upmanship.

Instead, the speculation surrounding her fate only intensified as a series of television documentaries tried to come up with an explanation. The first was broadcast by Thames Television in October 1975 and concentrated on the discovery of the lifebuoy. The two-part programme challenged the conclusion of the formal inquiry and suggested the lifebuoy had been deliberately planted by an unknown hand to conceal the true fate of the *Gaul*. With little or no real hard evidence to support its case, the programme went on to state the trawler must have either been captured by the Russians or struck by one of their submarines.

Other TV documentaries would follow similar lines even though the first real evidence of her final resting place was already starting to emerge. By 1977 several traces of a wreck in the area where the *Gaul* had last been seen were being reported by other fishing boats, leading to Government officials concluding there was more than a 50 per cent probability it was the missing trawler. Although this view was passed on to journalists at Thames Television and to some of the relatives, the focus would remain fixed on a possible Russian plot. In 1996 a Channel Four documentary was still saying much the same thing. Relying on previous incidents of collision between Nato and Warsaw Pact submarines, it suggested the *Gaul* had probably been sunk by a submarine and that this might have happened while the trawler was on a secret spying mission. 'Both Nato and the Russians have strongly and adamantly denied any responsibility but the evidence strongly suggests that she was sunk by a submarine,' said the programme. Once again, any actual evidence of a submarine strike was never produced as the wreck had yet to be found, but a year later the world would be watching grainy film footage of the long-lost trawler on the bed of the Barents Sea.

The efforts of TV producer Norman Fenton in discovering the *Gaul* would turn the mystery on its head. His dramatic underwater footage of the wreck could not shed any light on the submarine theory; indeed the trawler appeared relatively undamaged. However, the resulting Channel 4 *Dispatches* programme telling the story of the discovery detailed the known extent of trawlers being used to support spying activity during the 1950s and 1960s and obtained the admission from Lord Rodgers that he had been misled over the extent of the use of fishing vessels for this purpose. The programme also publicly named for the first time the supposed Hull-based 'spymaster' who had co-ordinated all this activity.

The late Commander John Brookes was suddenly hot news. The Hull West MP Alan Johnson attempted to shed more light on his role with a question in the House of Commons to Defence Secretary John Reid, asking for a statement on his role while in Hull. 'It is my department's policy to prevent the disclosure of information about any person (including a deceased person) or any other disclosure which could constitute or could facilitate an unwarranted invasion of privacy. I am, accordingly, withholding the information under exemption 14 of the Code of Practice to Access Government Information,' replied the Secretary of State. However, when Hull's local media asked the same question to former fishermen, they had no reservations about recalling the diminutive man from the Secret Intelligence Service and his office in the White Fish Authority building on St Andrew's Dock. While the *Dispatches* programme provided some detail, several ex-skippers produced cameras and observation cards provided by Brookes with which they were meant to record the movements of Russian military vessels. The cards even included helpful silhouettes of some of the warships they might come across.

Fenton's programme again rejected the notion that the *Gaul's* loss might have been caused by flooding in the factory deck caused by heavy seas. However, the re-opened public inquiry eventually concluded this was precisely the reason the trawler had foundered. Two subsequent Government-funded surveys of the wreck – ironically authorised by John Prescott in his new position as Deputy Prime Minister with a responsibility for transport issues – had carried out extensive filming with hi-tech, robot-controlled cameras being placed inside the vessel for the first time. In addition, limited human remains were also recovered. The pivotal finding from the second survey was the discovery that two chutes leading to the factory deck were fixed in an open position. Assuming they had been open at the time of her loss, the inquiry found the raging sea would have practically been invited inside the vessel with fatal results.

The Fenton expedition and the subsequent *Dispatches* programme not only persuaded Prescott to direct the Marine Accident Investigation Branch to carry out its own surveys of the wreck but also paved the way for a sharp U-turn by Defence Secretary John Reid over the whole issue of intelligence gathering by British trawlers during the Cold War. In a paper placed in the Library of the House of Commons, the Government finally gave a detailed account of what it described as the 'low-level intelligence' work involved in tracking the movements of the Soviet fleet over the best part of four decades. In doing so, it revealed just how misleading Bill Rodgers' letter to the Hull MPs had actually been some 14 years earlier. It said:

'As far as the United Kingdom was concerned the general collection of information on the activity of the Soviet fleet involved little more than reporting position and course and, where possible, photographing any vessel of potential interest. This is termed low-level intelligence. Such activity was carried out in international waters by anyone willing to do so. There is no evidence to say when such a practice began, but it represents a long tradition of support by the fishing fleet to the Royal Navy. While going about their business of fishing international waters, trawlermen volunteered such information as they thought right to report. This voluntary practice became more organised in the early 1960s with the issue of cameras to skippers if requested, and an established route for passing information to the appropriate authorities, the liaison office in Hull. In parallel with this voluntary assistance a scheme existed (dating back to Nelson's time) by which junior Royal Navy officers would gain valuable sea-going experience as well as fostering good relationships between fleets, by embarking on merchant vessels. Due to shortages of sea-going billets in the 1960s this scheme was extended to include deep sea trawlers. This scheme provided an added dimension to this low-level intelligence gathering activity, and all Royal Navy personnel embarked on fishing vessels were encouraged, in the same way as the trawler skippers had been doing, to report back sightings of interest.'

So instead of Rodgers' assertion that Royal Navy officers were simply there to learn about fishery protection work, it was now clear they had their eyes on something else. However, there were more revelations to come. The statement went on:

'Separate from the liaison scheme, and from an unknown date in the 1950s, personnel were occasionally embarked on trawlers with the specific aim of gathering intelligence whether by operation of passive radio listening equipment or visual sightings. This activity was conducted entirely on an opportunity basis, that is the trawler would go about its normal business, in an area of its choice, and sightings would be made by chance. Records do not indicate which vessels were used although it is believed that most, if not all, were owned by Boyd Line.By 1964 it was concluded that such deployment of manpower on an opportunity basis was not a particularly effective exercise as officers often spent weeks at sea following the cod to Iceland rather than working in more militarily interesting areas. It was therefore proposed that a trawler should be chartered for specific voyages in order to place specialist staff and equipment on board and to have some control over the area in which the vessel operated.'

The statement listed three such trips in three successive summers between 1965 and 1967 with the same trawler, the *Arctic Galliard* being used on each occasion. A specific guarantee was given to the skipper of the *Galliard* to compensate him for any resulting loss of catch, and records indicated the Royal Navy had paid out after two of the trips. The value of the intelligence work was equally disappointing and the chartered operations were abandoned.

However, the statement then referred to an operation carried out in early 1972 to recover a Soviet test missile which was believed to have landed in international waters in the Barents Sea. It turned out to be one of the two incidents mentioned by Lord Rodgers when Navy officers had supposedly joined a trawler to check radio navigation systems and look for what the then Defence Secretary had vaguely described as 'lost equipment'. It went on: 'It was agreed that a trawler, *Invincible,* would provide a more discreet means than a Royal Navy ship. To aid the search, satellite navigation equipment was fitted to the vessel. An RN officer was embarked, ostensibly to calibrate the satellite navigation system. The mission was unsuccessful. In September 1973 a similar mission was mounted. This time the trawler *Lord Nelson* was used. Again the operation was unsuccessful. This operation was the last recorded use of trawlers for specific intelligence gathering.'

The Government paper then turned to the *Gaul* and the many theories surrounding her possible use as a spy-ship at the time of her loss. As a relatively new vessel, it concluded the chances of any Royal Navy officer embarking on a so-called liaison trip on board the *Gaul* in the months leading up to its disappearance were remote. Although individual records for such voyages no longer existed, it was known that only ten junior officers had gone to sea on board Hull trawlers between 1969 and 1974. Satisfied with an acknowledgement made at the time by its owners, Hellyer Brothers, the Government confirmed there were no Royal Navy personnel on board the *Gaul* during its last voyage. It concluded: 'The involvement of trawlers in intelligence gathering was largely confined to the 1960s, albeit that two specific operations were mounted in 1972 and 1973. The passage of RN officers in the Barents Sea and North Cape similarly ceased by 1974 as a matter of policy. Records do not indicate when the passage of RN officers in trawlers generally ceased.'

If the statement delivered by John Reid finally lifted the lid on the secret if somewhat amateurish spying missions involving Hull trawlers during the Cold War, a curious footnote to the story was subsequently delivered at the re-opened formal investigation into the loss of the *Gaul* held in the city in early 2004. Hidden away in a separate room and giving evidence to the inquiry by audio-link, an MI6 officer, only referred to as Witness EB, told the hearing how he had searched through the archives of the Secret Intelligence Services to check whether there were any references to the *Gaul*. There were none. EB's testimony did, however, confirm the SIS activity detailed in the Reid statement and Commander Brookes' role as intelligence liaison officer in Hull between 1964 and 1971, as well as the fact that no permanent full-time replacement for him was ever appointed. Further titbits included instructions to skippers warning them not to enter into the 12-mile territorial zone operated by the Russians in their coastal waters and to jettison any 'compromising material' in the event of any encounter with a Russian craft.

The officer also confirmed the only incident recorded by the SIS after the decision in 1967 to stop using trawlers as spy-ships was a specific request by the Ministry of Defence for a trawler skipper to photograph Russian vessels in the course of a visit to a fishing exhibition in Leningrad. Like many before him. the skipper concerned was instructed to keep his mission secret from the rest of his crew. Ironically, the mate on that trip was Peter Nellist, who would subsequently be skipper on the *Gaul's* last voyage. Perhaps correctly, the inquiry concluded there was no evidence to suggest the *Gaul* or some members of her crew had been engaged in spying at the time of her loss. By 1974 the SIS had given up on the idea of relying on so-called 'low-level' intelligence operations by fishing trawlers, there were no official records relating to the *Gaul* or her previous guise as the *Ranger Castor,* and all the radio and electronic equipment identified onboard the *Gaul* from the film footage obtained during the 2002 survey was standard for a ship of her class at the time. However, the unprecedented acknowledgement that trawler crews from Hull had unknowingly been put at risk during up to 40 covert intelligence-gathering operations confirmed a much wider scandal which, thanks to the Cold War, remained hidden for decades.

Chapter 8

The Unmasking of a Double Agent

O N A WEDNESDAY AFTERNOON in July 1987 a middle-aged Palestinian cartoonist called Naji al-Ali was walking in a street close to the London offices of the Kuwaiti newspaper *Al Qabas International* where he worked, when he was confronted by a lone gunman who shot him in the head.

The 51-year-old was no stranger to danger, having lived in exile for most of his working life through a combination of invasion, censorship and threats issued as a result of his work. With no political affiliations, he had tried to represent ordinary Arab public opinion through his cartoons during an exceptionally volatile period of Middle-Eastern history. Few regimes or political groups escaped being featured in his satirical drawings, and while they often centred on the struggle and plight of the Palestinian people against Israeli occupation, he would infuriate both Arab and Jew, radical and conservative alike, by refusing to take sides.

Instead, his most famous character – a small boy called Hanzala who appeared as a spectator to the events in many of his best-known cartoons – came to represent his own views, inspired by his own childhood experiences in a Lebanese refugee camp. Explaining the character in an interview, he said: 'This child, as you can see, is neither beautiful, spoilt, nor even well-fed. He is barefoot like many children in refugee camps. He is actually ugly and no woman would wish to have a child like him. However, those who, like me, came to know 'Hanzala' later adopted him because he is affectionate, honest, outspoken, and a bum. He is an icon that stands to watch me from slipping. And his hands behind his back are a symbol of rejection of all the present negative tides in our region.'

Despite frequent arrests, censorship of his work and even death threats, Naji al-Ali became the highest-paid cartoonist in the Arab world. He was also said be one of the most wanted men in the Middle East, despised by those he ridiculed in print. Two weeks before the shooting he had been warned in a call from a friend, a senior member of the Palestinian Liberation Organisation in Tunisia, that his life was in danger as the result of a cartoon lampooning Egyptian journalist Rashida Muran, the official biographer of PLO leader Yasser Arafat. Naji al-Ali had infuriated Arafat in the past, notably in the mid-1970s when the PLO leader asked an audience of students during a visit to Kuwait if they knew of the cartoonist. 'Tell him if he doesn't stop drawing cartoons I will put his fingers in acid!' he told them.

With Naji al-Ali lying critically wounded in a London hospital, Scotland Yard's Anti-Terrorist Squad launched the hunt for the mystery gunman, who had fled from the scene before apparently disappearing. With Arafat's PLO under suspicion for ordering the shooting, detectives began re-tracing the last movements of Abdul Rahman Mustafa, a major in the PLO, who had hired a car in London on the afternoon of the shooting and then driven to a hotel in Stockport before checking out early the next morning. Manchester Airport, where the hire car was left, was just nine miles away. The police investigation in London led to a restaurant in Finchley thought to have been used by Mustafa before the shooting. A search of the building found personal papers and diaries belonging to the PLO man hidden in the loft. In one of the diaries was the name of Ismail Sowan and his address in Hull, where one of the most notorious international diplomatic scandals of the 1980s was about to unfold.

Two Scotland Yard officers travelled to Hull to co-ordinate their inquiries with local officers. They quickly established that Sowan had been on holiday in Israel at the time of the shooting and was therefore not considered to be a prime suspect. However, he still needed to be completely eliminated from the case. Carefully choosing the time to search his ground-floor flat to avoid attracting too much attention, the Anti-Terrorist Squad detectives and a handful of Hull officers arrived at the two-storey house masked by overgrown bushes and a hedge in Westbourne Avenue at 6.30am on 12 August. It was exactly four weeks since the shooting and Naji al-Ali was still on a hospital life-support machine.

Having returned from his holiday a few days earlier, Sowan was in the flat with his English wife Carmel when the police called. Initially, the small bed-sit flat seemed just like any other. Then the detectives found six locked suitcases in a bathroom cupboard. The first case opened by the Scotland Yard men contained nothing but holiday brochures and a medical book

Arab held in Hull arms raid 'Yard' squad

17 AUG 1987

VICTIM: Mr Ali Naji Awad Adhami

A 28-YEAR-OLD Arab is being held by Scotland Yard after anti-terrorist officers staged a dramatic arms swoop on a Hull flat.

The research assistant, who has not been named, was arrested by police probing the attempted assassination of an Arab cartoonist in London.

They recovered 68lb of high explosives said a Scotland Yard spokeswoman.

Included in the haul early last Wednesday morning were four assault rifles, seven hand grenades and bomb-making equipment featuring timers and clocks.

Magazines

Led by the Anti-Terrorist squad's Det. Alan Talbot, officers also recovered eight magazines loaded with 7.62mm of short ammunition and a large quantity of 38 and 9mm ammunition.

The Arab, who lives with his wife in Westbo... Hull, was detained under the Prevention... to Scotland Yard for further qu... in the raid.

The Arab wa... Londo...

Hull arms spy gets 11 years

AN ARAB spy found guilty of storing an arsenal of terrorist arms and explosives in Hull was jailed for 11 years at the Old Bailey today.

A double agent working for Israel to infiltrate the PLO, Ishmail Sowan kept the weapons in his bathroom cupboard.

The jury took just over three hours yesterday to decide that the Humberside college researcher knew of the arms cache in six locked suitcases given to him by a

By ANGUS YOUNG

PLO major he was tracking for the Israelis.

Passing sentence this morning, Mr Justice French said: "The offences of which you have been found guilty are of extreme gravity."

Appalling

Referring to last night's bomb attack in Northern Ireland, he added: "We were reminded only yesterday of the appalling uses to which materials such as those

mentioned here can be put. Deterrents and punishment are essential."

Sowan was given 11 years for possessing explosives and four years, to run concurrently, for possessing assault rifles.

The case is likely to spark a top-level political row over Israel's failure to inform Britain of the terrorist gang it was secretly storing in this country.

A senior anti-terrorist officer said: "The Israelis don't tell us anything."

Sowan (28) had been given the cases by Major Abdulrahman Mustapha before the PLO man fled the country last year after

the murder of an Arab cartoonist in London.

Described in court as a "ruthless, dedicated and sophisticated terrorist," Mustapha is a prime suspect as the mastermind behind that shooting.

Explosives

He made four separate trips to Sowan's Westbourne Avenue flat to deliver assault rifles, grenades, bomb making equipment and nearly 70lb. of high explosives.

The defence claimed Sowan was used by Mustapha whom he described in court as an "intelligent fox."

Flashback . . . police carry evidence away from the flat.

The naive loner with a secret

See Page 7.

but their suspicions were raised by something more sinister about the case itself – an empty hidden compartment hacked out of the foam filling. The second suitcase was to reveal the first of a series of shocking secrets. Inside was a tin packed with detonators and a plastic bag with wires attached to its covered contents. It was time to call in explosives experts from the Army.

The arsenal of weapons and explosives eventually recovered from the flat was staggering. Four rapid-fire AK47 assault rifles, eight magazines loaded with 300 rounds of ammunition, nine hand-grenades, bomb-making equipment and nearly 70lb of Semtex high explosives were all carefully removed for detailed forensic examination. Crucially, police also recovered a book about the 1982 war in Lebanon entitled *Flashback Beirut* from Sowan's flat. Featured in one of the book's photographs was Mustafa in a line-up of Palestinian leaders.

The haul stunned the Anti-Terrorist Squad officers, who had no prior intelligence to suggest Sowan was anything other than a name in Mustafa's contact book. The explosives found in the flat were nearly three times the amount used in the bombing of the Grand Hotel in Brighton three years earlier, when the IRA had tried to assassinate Prime Minister Margaret Thatcher and members of her cabinet. Had they been involved in an ordinary house fire, a large part of Westbourne Avenue would almost certainly have been blown to pieces.

Already under arrest, Sowan and his wife were taken to Scotland Yard for further questioning although she was subsequently released without charge. Sowan was eventually charged with unlawful possession of weapons and explosive substances. Meanwhile, after being in a coma for exactly five weeks, Naji al-Ali died.

Those who knew the softly spoken 28-year-old Jordanian from his work as a research assistant at Humberside College of Higher Education's School of Engineering in Queen's Gardens in the city centre were now coming to terms with the news that he was seemingly central to a major terrorism investigation. He had arrived in Hull 12 months earlier to start a two-year post at the college analysing the design of crankshafts in ship engines using advanced computer modelling, having previously studied in London. The research work was part of a bigger project on diesel-engine design being carried out by academics in Hull and Newcastle as well as experts from Lloyd's Register of Shipping.

Sowan's colleagues at the college revealed he was a talented but shy academic who appeared to be devoted to his research and his wife. 'He was no different from any other research worker,' said one. 'He was a model of consistency, hard-working and polite – even asking permission if he could leave early if he was going away for the weekend. There were several candidates for the job but it was felt he was the best suited to it with his academic credentials and ability.' Another colleague added: 'He was a quiet loner who would often work into the evening to solve a particular problem. He would never socialise and was quite private about his family. He never talked about life outside of college and would rarely volunteer information on himself or his plans for the future. The impression I got was that he wanted to stay in this country and his ambitions seemed to revolve around his wife.'

What his colleagues never knew and what the Scotland Yard detectives were about to discover was that Sowan had been leading an extraordinary secret life as an agent working for Mossad, Israel's intelligence service, having infiltrated a notorious PLO terrorist cell operating in Britain.

Details of his arrest in Hull were only made public six days after the event. Remarkably, despite the arrival of Army experts following the discovery of the hidden weapons and explosives, few neighbours had registered what might be happening literally on their doorsteps. As the news finally broke, the local media descended on Westbourne Avenue, hoping to find anyone who might have known Sowan and his wife. A woman who lived in another flat at the same address told reporters the brief extent of her dealings with him. 'I only ever saw him on two or three occasions, I had trouble understanding what he said but he seemed well-educated. He seemed quite a pleasant bloke from what I knew of him,' she said. At the rear of the house was the only clue to the drama from the week before – a dustbin full of special disposable white polythene zip-up suits used by police forensic scene-of-crimes officers. Eventually, the waiting photographers were rewarded for their patience by the arrival of two plain-clothes officers who had been sent to install a burglar alarm at the property which had suddenly became the centre of attention.

Back in London, the detectives quizzing Sowan slowly began to piece together a story straight out of the pages of an international spy thriller. At first he denied any knowledge of the weapons found in his flat and made no mention of his role with Mossad. After a week in custody, the detectives assigned to the case were still convinced he was actually working for the PLO. Then Sowan decided to reveal his true background.

During the course of a series of interviews, he told how he was first pressurised into joining a PLO faction as a teenager while studying for a civil engineering degree at university in Beirut. In the cloak-and-dagger world of Middle Eastern politics, he was then secretly recruited by Mossad, the Israeli secret service, who were initially keen to glean information about a PLO training course he had attended involving the use of guns and hand-grenades. Impressed by what he was able to report back to them, the Israelis then instructed him to rent a flat from one of their key targets, Abdul Mustafa.

Mustafa had already carved out a reputation for himself as one of the PLO's most dangerous figures. He belonged to Force 17, an elite corps given the task of providing a personal guard for PLO leader Yasser Arafat while also carrying out terrorist activities against Israel. One of Mustafa's operations had involved an attempted airliner hijacking in Munich when an Israeli passenger died after flinging himself over one of two hand-grenades which exploded during the attack. Sowan's undercover mission was to cultivate a friendship with Mustafa and feed useful details of his movements and contracts back to the Israelis. He made such a success of his assignment that the PLO officer would eventually act as the best man at his wedding. The young student's first undercover success was to lure a Palestinian arms dealer into an Israeli trap by posing as a would-be buyer. After graduating, he moved to Europe in 1982 to take up a language course in Paris. Regular payments from Mossad for information on the city's sizeable Palestinian population ensured he would never go hungry.

Two years later Sowan moved to the UK to start yet another engineering course, this time at Bath University. Once again, the Israelis kept him on their payroll after encouraging him to make contact with his former landlord Abdul Mustafa, who was also in the country working in the London offices of the Arab Defence League, a front group for the PLO. As in Paris, Mossad paid his rent and course fees together with £500 a month for his services. In 1986 Sowan married languages teacher Carmel Greensmith in London with Mustafa acting his best man. He told the police that she was completely unaware of his role as a spy or the true identity of the PLO man at her wedding. 'My wife did not know anything about the Israelis before we were married. I thought that was in the past. I was starting a new life,' he added.

In the same year Sowan moved to Hull, later telling police this was the time when he decided to end his work for the Israelis. Although he considered himself to be still on their books, he also claimed Mossad stopped paying him because they believed Hull was too far away from London for him to be of any real use to them. However, as far as Abdul Mustafa was concerned, Hull was the perfect place to set up a safe house.

In the early 1980s Force 17 along with other PLO units was forced to leave its headquarters in Lebanon after an Israeli attack. Moving to a new base in Tunisia, the unit began to expand its activities into Europe. The first step was to build an infrastructure of terrorist cells, weapon and ammunition depots and safe houses in various countries. One such cell, in Romania, was exposed when the authorities found a huge cache of arms in Bucharest in a house belonging to a Force 17 member.

Mustafa's role was to establish a Force 17 cell in the UK. Arriving in the country in 1983, he began weaving an intricate network of contacts that could be trusted to not only handle arms and explosives but keep them away from prying eyes. Although the British security services remained completely unaware of the PLO cell, Mossad was receiving sporadic information on Mustafa from Sowan. In the summer of 1986 Mustafa bought a petrol station in Essex for £26,000, paying £16,000 immediately in cash with money provided by the PLO. The garage in Leigh-on-Sea was to become an unlikely UK outpost for Arafat's organisation, providing the perfect cover for Mustafa to embark on a recruitment campaign. Police would later conclude that a 14-strong team under his direction was behind the murder of Naji al-Ali. By early 1987 Mustafa began making plans to leave the UK for Cyprus, telling friends he was facing bankruptcy. In fact, it was a deliberate cover story to prepare for a more necessary departure once the cartoonist had been killed. Sowan's move to Hull also provided Mustafa with the perfect opportunity to leave his arms cache in a safe but distant pair of hands. The PLO man made a total of four trips to Hull, bringing the suitcases packed with guns and explosives with him. Three of the journeys took place in March, a month before his planned departure to Cyprus. When he suddenly re-appeared unannounced in Westbourne Avenue four months later, even Sowan was surprised. Mustafa claimed he was back in the UK to sort out the details of his house sale. In reality, he had returned to put the finishing touches to the assassination plot.

Although revealing his role with Mossad to the astonished Scotland Yard team, Sowan insisted he knew nothing about the true contents of the suitcases. Instead, he claimed Mustafa had told him they contained nothing but clothes and an electrical answering-machine. He stuck to the same story during his trial, held amid tight security at the Old Bailey in London in June 1988, where he pleaded not guilty to the unlawful possession of four assault rifles and unlawful possession of explosive substances. However, during his evidence, he revealed for the first time that his Israeli spymasters had told him they knew Mustafa was involved with a substantial arms store somewhere in the country. 'At the time I thought the Israelis were imagining things, they are always doing that,' he told the jury. Recalling his arrest, he added: 'At that moment I felt I was under pressure and I felt betrayed by everybody. I was feeling guilty putting innocent people in trouble, such as my wife and her family.' Speaking in fluent English, Sowan also revealed that despite the years spent cultivating his friendship with Mustafa he believed the PLO man never really fully trusted him. 'The Israelis said Mustafa had something in this country. They told me in 1985. They wanted me to find out about it. They believed he had weapons stored in this country,' he said. When asked by police if he thought it was odd that a senior figure in the PLO should leave a cache of arms with someone he distrusted, he replied: 'He must have been mad.'

His defence counsel, Mr David Cochs QC, attempted to pin the blame on Mustafa. 'He knew Sowan could be used as a mug to store property which contained these explosives,' he said in his closing remarks. The jury, however, sided with the prosecution's argument that Sowan knew perfectly well that his flat was being used as secret arms dump and took just three hours to find him guilty on both charges. Sentencing him to 11 years in prison, Mr Justice French told Sowan: 'The offences of which you have been found guilty are of extreme gravity.' Referring to a bomb attack in Northern Ireland on the previous evening, he added: 'We were reminded only yesterday of the appalling uses to which materials such as those mentioned here can be put. Deterrents and punishment are essential.'

Giving evidence during the trial, Anti-Terrorist Squad Detective Inspector William MacMurry had named Mustafa as the prime suspect in the killing of Naji al-Ali, yet nearly a year on from the shooting he was no closer to being brought to justice, having fled abroad to an unknown hiding. Subsequently, no one was ever charged with the cartoonist's murder.

With the trial over, the inevitable diplomatic row exploded but even now it remains unclear who was really telling the truth about the affair. Britain's secret service organisations let it be known they were furious that Israel had ignored the usual protocol for Western intelligence organisations to share information on covert operations being mounted in other countries. Typically, this arrangement allows agents to work from their respective embassies while the host country is kept informed of their activities. However, in Sowan's case, the British authorities publicly claimed Mossad had kept them completely in the dark over the tracking of Mustafa and his arms cache and its attempts to infiltrate the PLO cell. Prime Minister Thatcher duly wrote a letter of protest to the Israeli Prime Minister Yitzhak Shamir and expelled two Israeli diplomats together with three Mossad men from London. Mossad would subsequently be forced to relocate its entire UK operation to Belgium in what many regarded as a humiliating move.

Some intelligence experts were convinced the case was one of the most embarrassing episodes in Mossad's history. The detailed exposure of a secret service operation was bad enough but the Old Bailey trial had guaranteed worldwide publicity. The Israelis' apparent mistakes in failing to inform their British counterparts about the suspected arms cache and allowing Sowan to return to Britain from a holiday in Israel and into the arms of the Scotland Yard were regarded as almost schoolboy errors.

However, others saw it differently. In his 1991 book *The Intelligence Game,* author James Rusbridger came to an alternative conclusion. He suggested Mossad's plan was to get Sowan to let off the bombs in Britain, leaving sufficient forensic clues to suggest they were the work of Arab extremists, thus damaging Anglo-Arab relations. At the time there was talk of Britain re-establishing links with Syria, while Britain had also just concluded a lucrative contract to sell aircraft and military equipment to Saudi Arabia. According to Rusbridger, Israel was keen to show that Arab countries were not to be trusted. He claimed Sowan had been 'run' by a five-man Mossad team under the cover of a private company with the tacit approval of the Foreign Office and MI5 because in return Mossad was giving useful information to MI6 about Middle East terrorist groups and hostages held in Lebanon. When the operation suddenly became unexpectedly public, the Foreign Office was left with no choice but to expel the two Israeli diplomats and order Mossad to leave.

What was not reported subsequently was Mossad's own retaliation. Stung by Britain's actions, the Israelis told MI6 that the exchange of information about terrorists and hostages was at an end. Rusbridger claims MI6 was horrified at this and warned MI5 that it was getting far more information from Mossad than it was giving the Israelis. After pressure was put on the Foreign Office, it was quietly agreed that a Mossad undercover team could return to work in Britain.

Sowan was eventually deported just before Christmas in 1992, having served six years in prison. Armed police escorted him from the top security Full Sutton jail near Pocklington to Heathrow Airport, where a seat on a flight to Israel was awaiting him.

According to one national newspaper at the time, an anonymous friend claimed he was not looking forward to being released. The friend, who had reportedly visited Sowan in prison, said: 'He is absolutely terrified of going back to Israel because he believes he will be killed. His brother was kidnapped four years ago and he thinks the same fate awaits him. He feels abandoned and betrayed.'

The report claimed prison visits by the Israeli authorities stopped within his first year behind bars. The same applied to his wife, who eventually broke off all contact and applied for a divorce. There is no record of what did happen after he stepped off the plane in Israel. Perhaps the truth about Ismail Sowan and his time in Hull will never be known.

Chapter 9
Trouble at the Top

A<small>T SOME POINT OR OTHER</small>, many of the scandals in this book feature police investigations into allegations of wrong-doing and criminal behaviour. Typically, the matters in question end up being tried and tested by the judicial system with varying outcomes for those concerned. But what happens when the police themselves are the focus of scandal? In the cases of two Chief Constables of Hull, the courts were never troubled but two prominent careers were brought to undignified ends.

James Campbell was only the third person to hold the title of Chief Constable of Hull. Having previously been employed by the North East Railway Company in York as a police superintendent, he was appointed to the post in late 1880 after being chosen from a shortlist of six candidates by the watch committee.

Part of Hull Corporation, the committee had been formed some 44 years earlier after legislation gave powers to municipal authorities to create new-style police forces. Until then, the system of policing in Hull and most other sizeable towns had remained largely unchanged since the Middle Ages, with unpaid parish constables and watchmen responsible for arresting offenders and taking them before magistrates. They were overseen by a high constable but this position was usually as vague as the talents of the men he was nominally in charge of, most of whom were regarded as unemployable in any other trade or calling and often susceptible to bribery and drunkenness.

Hull's rapid expansion as a trading port and the advent of the industrial revolution meant change was inevitable, not least because the population was growing rapidly. When new legislation prompted a review of the town's existing system of parish watches at least half of the 102 watchmen were found to be totally unfit for duty. Ten were over the age of 60 and another 48 were over 50, while only four of the

96 parish constables were considered to be fully active.

Improved policing regimes in other large towns, including the use of 24-hour shift systems, was driving criminals to Hull in search of an easier life and richer pickings. The review recommended the creation of a new police force of 110 men covering four districts and a new watch committee to govern it. All of the new officers would be paid and given a uniform, while the committee would employ a full-time clerk.

Alexander McManus was appointed Hull's first Chief Constable, although initially he led the new-look police force as a superintendent. A firm disciplinarian, he spent 30 years at the helm and during that time became one of the town's leading and most respected figures. His successor, Thomas Cooke, fared less well. A visit to Hull by Her Majesty's Inspector of Constabulary in 1875 uncovered irregularities in the way Cooke handled certain accounts, notably money he received from licences issued by the police to street traders and chimney sweeps as well as funds reserved for pensions, the police band and the force library. A subsequent investigation by the watch committee found Cooke was taking cuts from a range of fees, including money paid by parents of children committed to reform schools. Having risen through the ranks during the McManus era to eventually become Chief Constable, Cooke had no option but to resign when the committee's damning report was published and the search began for a successor.

At first, James Campbell appeared to be just what the members of the watch committee were looking for. Unlike Cooke, he was not an internal promotion so he arrived in Hull without any damaging connections with the previous postholder or the local police force. He also enjoyed a reputation as a tough, no-nonsense upholder of the law who set high standards for behaviour not only on the streets of Hull but also within the ranks of his own force, writing its first-ever training manual. When an officer fell foul of the law, Campbell took a firm line and regularly clashed with the members of the watch committee who tended to be more lenient.

His annual report presented to the committee for the year ending 30 September 1885 captures Campbell at the peak of his powers and provides a fascinating snapshot of the policing of crime in late Victorian Hull. During the preceding 12 months Campbell's force had issued proceedings against 7,087 people and secured 6,358 convictions. Out of that total, there were 785 cases of drunkenness, 117 assaults on the police and 854 breaches of the peace. His report highlights an increase in the total number of prosecutions under the Lord's Day Act, covering activities being carried out on a Sunday – up from 1,900 in the previous year to 2,028 – and a total of 300 cases still classed as undetected, the vast majority recorded as 'simple larcenies from clothes lines, shops, etc, valued at five shillings and upwards.'

The report also covers the annual cost of policing in Hull, at a time when the force itself had more than doubled from its original size under McManus to a total of 277 officers under Campbell. Salaries accounted for four-fifths of the gross total of just under £26,000, up £5,000 on the previous year, thanks in part to the recently opened new police station in Gordon Street in west Hull, as well as the issuing of new top coats, capes and leggings to every officer.

Campbell was also assiduous in keeping the watch committee up to date with important changes in national legislation which had a direct impact on Hull. The 1885 Criminal Law Amendment Act was a case in point, prompting the Chief Constable to deliver a detailed report on the implications of strengthening the laws against prostitution while offering new protection for women and young girls in cases of sexual assault. The Act raised the age of consent from 13 to 16 years of age, made it a criminal offence to procure girls for prostitution by administering drugs, punished householders for permitting under-age sex on their premises and provided new powers to issue summary proceedings to be taken against brothels.

In his report to the committee, Chief Constable Campbell focused almost exclusively on the Act's references to the age of consent and the policing of brothels, reflecting the considerable local and national concern over the two issues. He failed to mention a clause which re-criminalised male homosexuality of any kind in what was almost certainly a deliberate omission reflecting the moral climate of the day. Any public reference to homosexuality was largely frowned on by the Victorians.

'There can be no doubt that this Act of Parliament will prove one of the most important enactments affecting the criminal law and the protection of women and young girls generally, which has been placed on the Statue for many years past,' he said.

On the question of brothels, Campbell gave his only personal observation in an otherwise straightforward summary of most of the new powers within the Act: 'Under the old system it was necessary that the particular prosecution should take place at Quarter Sessions or at the Assizes, but powers are now given to magistrates to deal with cases summarily in petty sessions, a fine of £20 or three months' imprisonment being incurred for the first offence. The only difficulty which at present exists is as to whether the statute empowers the police to lodge informations and secure convictions upon evidence by themselves alone, legal opinion being divided upon that point. I may say, however, that I am at present in communication with the Public Prosecutor who has promised to forward me with a definite reply to the question I have raised shortly.'

Already known as something of a moral crusader, it is likely that Campbell would have relished the police being given the opportunity to pursue a new crackdown against brothels through their own means without the obvious difficulties in having to obtain supporting evidence from often unwilling regular customers. He added: 'I can only add in conclusion my belief that, with the co-operation of the public and the police, the Act cannot fail to have a very beneficial effect, especially in protecting young girls and I have every confidence that the Hull Police Force will not fail to enforce its provisions in the future.'

His report was duly accepted by the committee members, who no doubt looked forward to a renewed drive to clean up some of Hull's seedier streets, where prostitution and brothel-keeping were endemic. What none of the committee probably expected was a new scandal involving their Chief Constable and a 14-year-old girl at an address in one of those very streets.

By the time the watch committee gathered in the Town Hall for its scheduled meeting on 18 November, allegations about the behaviour of the Chief Constable were already circulating. They were almost certainly triggered by the highly charged atmosphere created by an impending General Election, the first to be held since Hull was divided into three separate parliamentary constituencies. Voting in the three-week polling period was not scheduled to get underway until November 24, but the candidates' campaigns were well underway and indiscretions of any kind associated with those involved were being seized on by their opponents.

As Chief Constable, Campbell was tasked with ensuring the election ran smoothly but he was not without his enemies in certain sections of Hull's political elite. Having publicly challenged some of the watch committee's decisions on disciplinary matters involving some of his own officers, he was not universally popular with some on the Corporation.

The secret war

NEARLY 50 years ago, a storm exploded in war-time Hull when a councillor made a shocking allegation of bribery and harassment in the city's police force.

When outspoken Coun Alfred Kyno Jacobs apparently withdrew his allegations a week later, that was just the start of a controversy which rocked the city for years.

For the controversial Coun Jacobs was later to claim the equally colourful Chief Constable Thomas "Tosh" Wells had tricked him into withdrawing his accusations.

He was also to claim Mr Wells had been trying to sabotage his reputation as his political rivals, Aldermen Leo Schultz and Archibald Stark.

And when he eventually made an official complaint about Mr Wells' conduct, Jacobs' accusations were passed to the Home Secretary who launched an investigation.

But the allegations and details of the subsequent Home Office inquiry have only just been released after 45 years, after the row was raised again in a book about Hull's police by former Humberside Deputy Chief Constable Tony Clarke.

The row eventually resulted in Mr Wells resigning from the old city force in 1947 on the grounds of ill health, but the details and the ground to the feud remained sec...

Results of a Government investigation into the activities of a former Chief Constable of Hull have finally come to light after nearly 50 years of secrecy. The papers were pronounced so secret that they were to be kept under lock and key for 80 years under a tough Government ruling. But pressure from the Mail finally brought them to light.

Reporter **Melanie Hannam** was able to delve into a mysterious feud between the city's top policeman and an outspoken councillor.

It was a simple statement made by Coun Jacobs in a city council meeting that acted as a catalyst to a controversy that had been bubbling under the surface almost since Mr Wells' appointment as Chief Constable in 1941.

Jacobs caused a furore by claiming the police had been following him about following someone and had offered someone £50 if he offered a bribe.

"The money would be paid if the right person was there in a court case, that Coun Jacobs had accepted a bribe but this was the allegation Coun Jacobs was to make at...

... councillor had earned commission from the deal. And he was also to allege that the dealer had been offered £50 if he would testify Jacobs had accepted a bribe.

The councillor maintained the police were only being strenuous in denying they had ever tried to bribe the dealer.

This was the allegation Coun Jacobs was to make at...

...in which members of the police authority learned of Jacobs' retreat, a statement was issued to the Press. This left Coun Jacobs feeling his public image had been compromised.

Mr Raphael summed up the political climate in Hull in the 1940s in his report.

"It was Mr Wells' misfortune that he took up his appointment in Hull at a time when the Council and, in particular, the Watch Committee, were divided into factions, involving the bitterest hostility," he said.

But Mr Wells did not keep aloof from the warring factions. For example, the Chief Constable had installed an apparatus in his office just to record his conversations with Coun Jacobs.

Coun Jacobs made the five official accusations against Mr Wells:

● In November, 1942, the Chief Constable allowed one of his officers to visit Mr Jacobs' office for a reason other than police business. Basically, the councillor claimed one of Mr Wells' detectives visited him twice solely to "persecute" him by suggesting he had been goods in his possession.

...n January 1944, the Chief Constable had canvassed Coun Jacobs regarding a matter relating to...

War-time secrets revealed
11 JAN 1993

DETAILS of a sensational feud between two of Hull's top war-time officials were made public today after decades of secrecy. Papers on former Chief Constable of Hull, Thomas "Tosh" Wells, were to have remained secret until the next century under Government secrecy rules.

The report is a Home Office investigation which was launched...

Secret file on top cop

THE RESULTS of a Government investigation into the activities of a former Chief Constable of Hull will remain shrouded in secrecy until the next century.

The papers on Chief Constable Thomas "Tosh" Wells (left) are still under lock and key after he resigned from the old city police force on health grounds until 2027.

The 80-year secret has been revealed in a new book by a former Humberside Deputy Chief Constable Tony Clark.

Mr Clark wrote to the Home Office asking when the Wells inquiry papers but was refused.

"I asked them why but they would not say," said Mr Clarke.

"He was supposed to have investigated for misusing police vehicles and for misusing police..."

... after it makes you wound what ...they may have found out. Said to be ...later the time of his retirement in 1947, Mr Wells lived until 1967, dying at the age of 70.

All confidential government...

...the councillor to withdraw accusations that police had tried to frame Mr Wells and were harassing him.

The inquiry, headed by Home Office-appointed Mr Geoffrey Raphael concluded that Mr Wells had broken his code of conduct.

"A combination of personal animosity and muddled thinking, by no means on one side only, has led to serious infractions of the code of conduct which is properly required of the head of a police force," said Mr Raphael, who went on to praise Mr Wells.

● Report special see page 4

...papers are kept secret for 30 years, but especially sensitive ones, particularly referring to intelligence work or military trials, can be work or military. The papers regarding the arrest of leading Nazi Rudolph Hess were released last year after 50 years and the Suez Crisis papers came out after 30 years.

West Hull MP Stuart Randall called the situation about "Tosh" Wells papers "nonsensical".

"To keep these papers secret in...

...1992 is nothing short of absurd," he added.

A Home Office spokeswoman was unable to shed any light on the 80-year disclosure rule but said it was standard practice.

Mr Wells arrived from Chesterfield in 1941. An able policeman, Wells was notorious for his eccentric behaviour. He ran into trouble with "Kyno" politician Coun Alfred Kyno Jacobs. The two became bitter enemies.

● See Flashback: Page 6, Comment: Page 30 and...

ACCUSED: Former Chief Constable Thomas "Tosh" Wells. Details of a Home Office inquiry into his conduct have only just been released after 45 years.

96

His firm views on law and order were also at odds with many Liberal-leaning figures in the town. A political connection to the scandal about to erupt around him was never established but the coincidence of the election campaign is hard to ignore.

It started when a woman contacted the Mayor, John Willows, in his role as a magistrate, asking for his advice on whether she should submit a formal complaint about Campbell's behaviour towards her daughter during a visit to their home. The girl in question was Edith Ann Creighton, a 14-year-old who lived with her family in St Thomas Place, off Portland Street in the town centre. When Campbell was subsequently told about the mother's meeting with the Mayor he returned to the house to ask about her allegations against him. Later the same day he visited Mrs Creighton again, accompanied by a clerk from his solicitor's office. If those two visits were designed to head off trouble for the Chief Constable they failed spectacularly. A day letter he was forced to write a letter to the watch committee. It read: 'Gentlemen, you are no doubt aware that a serious charge has been preferred against me, with which the public have become familiar. I have taken the earliest opportunity in my power of giving a positive and emphatic denial to the charge, and of requesting a full enquiry into the matter; and, pending such investigation, I feel that the proper course is to leave myself entirely in the hands of the committee, which I beg respectfully to do. I am, gentlemen, your obedient servant, Jas. Campbell, Chief Constable.'

The task of investigating the Chief Constable was given to the watch committee rather than Campbell's own police force, after the Corporation's town clerk decided that a lack of corrobative evidence in the case would make any attempted prosecution almost impossible. It was also noted that the girl's mother had no intention of taking any proceedings against him. As a result, a special sub-committee of three – the chairman, deputy chairman and town clerk – was formed to examine the matter in detail and interview the three main participants – Edith Creighton, her mother and Campbell – while they were all in the same room.

The girl told how she was alone in the house on the night of 13 November. At the time, her father was away at sea while her mother and a girl who lodged with them had been attending a temperance meeting in the town. Her 13-year-old brother, who would have normally been there, had not returned from work when the Chief Constable arrived shortly after seven o'clock.

According to Edith, Campbell kissed her when he entered the house and asked if her mother was in. She told him about the meeting and said she could go out and bring her back to the house if necessary, but he said it did not matter. The girl then claimed Campbell asked whether anyone could see into the house through the window-blind before she volunteered to close some shutters. Campbell then sat in a chair, asked her to sit on his knee, put his arm around her waist and kissed her, telling her how she had grown since he had last seen her. Edith then claimed the Chief Constable asked her to show him her leg and pulled her clothes right up to her knee. She said Campbell asked her to kiss him and say that she loved him and she admitted kissing him. He then told her to kiss him again and she did on the side of the face. At this, he told her to kiss him again on the mouth and as she did so he put his tongue into her mouth. She told the sub-committee she thought he meant something by doing this because he later asked if anyone had kissed her like that before.

The teenager claimed Campbell then let her get off his knee allowing her to move to the other side of a table At this point she said she saw him unbuttoning his trousers before he called her to come to him and say that she loved him. She stood her ground and he backed off. He then produced a sixpence, gave it to Edith and told her not to tell her mother that he had called. The girl said she should inform her mother about the visit and, according to her, he replied: 'You can tell her I have called, and if I can assist her I will,' before adding, 'You won't tell her anything else?' and 'You are vexed with me, aren't you?' After he left, Edith locked the front door leaving the key in a place where she knew her mother would find it and went to bed afraid that he would return. Cross-examined by the sub-committee, she said she had not called out for help during his visit because she knew he was the Chief Constable and she was frightened of him. The following day she told two friends at the warehouse where she worked about Campbell's visit and they advised her to tell her mother. When Mrs Creighton was informed, she decided to approach the Mayor's office.

Campbell was also given the chance to cross-examine Edith but she stuck rigidly to her account of what had happened between them. It was then the Chief Constable's turn to give his version of events. He confirmed his visit to the house and admitted sitting Edith on his knee and kissing her once on the cheek. He also acknowledged he had talked about her legs, claiming he had simply patted her on the shins without lifting the girl's dress before talking generally about her family. Campbell strenuously denied the other accusations made against him, suggesting they had been made up.

The sub-committee's subsequent report concluded that Campbell's reasons for going to the house in the first place were perfectly satisfactory – he had known the family for several years and was in the habit of giving coppers and, on one occasion, a threepenny piece, to Edith and her brother. Closing the shutters was another habit which the sub-committee accepted was perfectly normal, as was the Chief Constable's assertion that he had kissed the girl on previous visits to the house in the presence of her mother and brother without any fuss being made of it. As a father of nine himself, he said he was affectionate with all children.

However, Mrs Creighton's evidence was telling. She gave details of Campbell's two subsequent visits to the house to see her. She claimed he pleaded with her not to allow Edith to appear before the sub-committee because it would ruin him. Instead, he suggested she go to the police court and say it was all a mistake and that his kindness towards her daughter had been misunderstood.

If the Chief Constable had hoped to clear his name, the full watch committee's decision to hear the case in public almost certainly sealed his fate. Reporters from rival newspapers eagerly devoured the evidence laid out in the sub-committee report and then faithfully recorded an address by the Chief Constable, who once again declared his innocence. Edith Creighton was also called to give evidence, answering a number of questions from members of the committee. They then withdrew to allow the committee time to consider its decision. When it came the motion requesting Campbell to tender his resignation as Chief Constable was unanimous.

Faced with little option, Campbell agreed to resign. After a short debate, the committee accepted his request to be paid three months' salary to help his large family adjust to his dramatically changed circumstances. Hull's newspapers were divided over whether he deserved to be forced out or not. Many pointed out that nothing had actually been proven, while others recalled recent examples of leniency by the watch committee towards other high-ranking police officers who had admitted various financial irregularities, all of whom had received lesser punishment. Even so, some argued that working relations between Campbell and the committee had been fragile for some time and it was best that he should go sooner rather than later. With his reputation in ruins, Campbell and his family emigrated to Australia after the cost of their journey was raised by some of his remaining supporters.

If Campbell's fall from grace was played out very much in the public eye, another Chief Constable's highly unusual departure from the post was conducted under the tightest of secrecy. In fact, the true story behind the early retirement of Thomas Wells in 1947 would remain hidden in a classified Home Office file for an astonishing 44 years.

Arriving from a senior police post in Chesterfield, Wells was appointed Chief Constable in 1941 when Hull was suffering some of the worst bombing of the Second World War. It was a pivotal moment in the city's history and arguably the last time genuine fears were being expressed about the possibility of an invasion by a foreign power.

Police recruitment had been halted since the outbreak of hostilities and all officers under the age of 30 had been drafted into the Armed Forces. In their place, the First Police Reserve was formed to maintain law and order. The Reserve mainly consisted of men over 30-years-old who still had other jobs, their reward for acting as reserve policemen being regular pay while on duty. Retired policemen were also encouraged to rejoin what eventually became the Police War Reserve. They might have been the police equivalent of Dad's Army, but the reserve would play a vital role in Hull's war effort when enemy air-raids left over 1,000 dead, 100,000 homeless and vast areas of the city in ruins.As well as normal policing duties, they were tasked with carrying out observation work during air-raids and dangerous rescue missions from the remains of shattered buildings alongside fire and ambulance crews. Eight police and fire officers lost their lives during bombing raids, including an assistant chief constable.

The understandably unstable nature of the police force during the war years reflected Wells' own personality. He quickly developed a reputation as someone who was prepared to bend the rules if it suited him, while his close friendships with some of the leading figures in Hull's boxing circles raised eyebrows among those who believed the sport was just one jab away from the world of organised crime. Wells became an enthusiastic promoter of charity boxing shows and was the driving force behind the creation of the Hull City Police Boys' Club in 1943. Concerned about the lack of facilities for young boys and the dearth of parental supervision caused by fathers being away on the frontline and mothers working long hours, Wells had noticed juvenile crime was rising fast. His idea was to overhaul a former gentlemen's club set up for residents of Garden Village and turn it into a boys' boxing club for 10- to 18-year-olds. The club proved to be a runaway success with 150 boys enrolling on the first day.

As the war dragged on, stories about Wells' unconventional behaviour started to seep out from the force. Tales of backhanders, favouritism and pulling rank abounded. One tale involved him organising unauthorised supplies of strictly rationed food for his staff and personal friends outside the force. Another featured a clash with a startled gamekeeper who came across the unlikely sight of the Chief Constable of Hull standing on the shoulders of his official driver while attempting to cut down a Christmas tree in a forest on a country estate. Wells was also known to like a drink, regularly turning up worse for wear at the force's garage late at night after a social function before ordering someone to drive him home.

Although appointed by the watch committee, Wells soon clashed with some of its leading figures as well as others on the city council. Among those who took a dim view of the some of the rumours surrounding the Chief's behaviour was Alderman Alfred Jacobs, himself a notoriously prickly character with a reputation for taking no prisoners when it came to speaking out against those who he believed to be in the wrong.

A member of the Municipal Association Group at the Guildhall, Jacobs was not afraid of making enemies even among his own council colleagues. In 1934 he was taken to court by the city's valuation officer Douglas Boyd, who sued him for slander over statements he made about the official's professional capacity. Jacobs was unable to substantiate his claims about Boyd and was advised to settle the action by making a public apology and paying a sum to cover damages and costs.

In 1943 he was involved in another slander case, this time as the plaintiff taking an action against Alderman Archibald Stark. A Labour stalwart and former Lord Mayor, Stark had been awarded an OBE the previous year in recognition of his work as commandant of the civilian Hull Auxiliary Fire Service during the worst of the bombing raids on the city. Having been the city's first volunteer fire-fighter at the start of the war, Stark made a personal point of turning out with his civilian crews during every raid and once narrowly escaped death after being blown off his feet during an incident in Lime Street.

Stark's reputation as a political heavyweight and his standing as leader of the Labour group cut little ice with Jacobs, although what turned out to be a long-running rivalry between the two men also owed much to their very different backgrounds. A boilermaker and committed Socialist,

Stark threw himself into the struggle to establish the Labour Party in Hull after the end of the First World War and achieved some local notoriety during the 1926 General Strike when he was jailed for three months after being involved in an incident involving striking tramway workers who blocked a bus on Holderness Road in contravention of emergency laws brought in to counter strike action. In contrast, Jacobs was a self-made businessman with strong Conservative leanings despite the official title of his Municipal group.

The slander case was triggered by an earlier internal council inquiry into the conduct of another councillor in the hiring of lorries for the Auxiliary Fire Service. Although the inquiry found nothing against the councillor concerned, Jacobs was not satisfied with the outcome and continued to pursue the matter. As a self-employed motor dealer, he had more than a passing interest in the hiring and buying of vehicles by the council. It led him to make a speech at a full council meeting attacking Stark in his role as AFS commandant. In return, Stark blasted back with both barrels and effectively accused Jacobs of indulging in disreputable business practices.

'This is one of the biggest and most important factors which makes him take his action,' Stark told the meeting, with Jacobs firmly in his sights. 'I had about 160 cars to buy (for the council) and I said: "Jacobs is not touching them". I could see into the future that buying cars is like horse-dealing. Unless you are an expert you are likely to be tricked.' Although his words were jumbled, their meaning could not have been clearer, at least to Jacobs. Stark was claiming he was a dishonest trickster who couldn't be trusted when it came to buying and selling vehicles. Stark, however, went further in his speech. He recalled the Boyd case eight years earlier when he had been Lord Mayor. He told how, at the time, Jacobs had approached him with a letter which had apparently been stolen from a company safe purporting to show evidence of the valuation officer's corruption. According to Stark, Jacobs had asked him to read the letter out at the next council meeting and offered him £200 if he agreed. When he refused, Stark claimed Jacobs told him he was a fool to refuse the opportunity to earn £200 for two minutes' work.

The slander hearing at Leeds Assizes court also heard allegations of another exchange between the two councillors in 1938, when Stark claimed Jacobs had asked him in his capacity as chairman of the watch sub-committee to cut him into a council contract for two new police saloon cars. Again Stark said Jacobs had offered him a bribe – this time £30 – which he again turned down. When Jacobs threatened to move a motion against the sub-committee's minutes authorising the contract to a rival motor firm, Stark shrugged it off. Giving evidence at the hearing, he prompted laughter in the court when asked what Jacobs did then. 'Nothing, He never does, he sits in a corner and issues writs,' he replied.

Stark's speech left the judge little alternative but to find in Jacobs' favour, although he went further by claiming the Labour councillor had deliberately tried to ruin Jacobs' career by calling him a trickster and accusing him of offering bribes. There was no evidence, he contended, of truth in the slanders. With the two councillors sticking firmly to their own versions of what one said to the other in private, and in the absence of anyone else being present at the time, Stark's very public comments in his speech provided the only real evidence.

However, the judge also acknowledged Jacobs' reputation as a self-appointed *agent provocateur*. 'He is obviously an extremely unpopular man on Hull City Council and, according to one speaker at a meeting, he is a man of whom some members are afraid. He is unpopular because he is always on the look-out for what he considers is wrong doing. He accepts the position; in fact he is rather proud of it. In his view there is a lot going on in the council which he thinks should not go on.' The judge said he was inclined to accept it was also quite likely that Jacobs also made complaints about things which did not merit a complaint in the first place. In this regard, he said Jacobs was a 'perpetual nuisance', who was quite content to have such a reputation.

Stark was ordered to pay £175 damages as well as costs but could at least rely on support from the current Lord Mayor, Leo Schultz, a trusted Labour colleague and a sworn enemy of Jacobs. During the hearing, Schultz had given evidence firmly backing Stark's version of events. He also brushed off suggestions from Jacobs' barrister that his hostility towards his client had been triggered by Jacobs' decision not to appoint Schultz as his company secretary and accountant several years earlier. Schultz denied any ill-feeling towards Jacobs while admitting to doing all he could to prevent him playing a leading role in a re-organisation of the casualty section of the city's civil defence.

Against this background of tit-for-tat political backbiting, writs and stitch-ups, the behaviour of Chief Constable Wells only added fuel to the fire. Inevitably, Jacobs started to take an interest in Wells' apparently liberal use of what were supposed to be strictly rationed petrol allowances. He was certain the Chief was using far more fuel supplies for his own car than the force was officially allowed and, through the watch committee, succeeded in even having the use of the vehicle temporarily suspended. A subsequent inquiry by the Minister of Fuel and Petrol concluded it was satisfied 'there was no impropriety' in the use of the Chief Constable's car and Wells was cleared. However, a deeply personal feud between the two men had only just begun.

Wells struck back by starting his own investigations into Jacobs, who would later claim the Chief's pursuit of him was aided and abetted by his two main political foes, his old adversaries Alderman Stark and Alderman Schultz. In particular, Wells ordered detectives to look into the circumstances surrounding the council's purchase of a lorry from a firm near Pontefract. It turned out that Jacobs had originally seen the vehicle and had suggested to its owner that the council might be interested in buying it. The company's boss eventually approached the council and the sale was completed. Several months later, however, Jacobs learned that police officers had visited the firm to ask if the councillor had earned any commission from the deal. They came away without any evidence to suggest Jacobs had acted improperly. He would later claim the Pontefract motor dealer had been offered £50 by the police if he would testify that he had accepted a bribe.

Relations between Wells and Jacobs continued to be difficult. Some months after the Pontefract investigation, the councillor was visited at his home by another detective. It wasn't a social call, explained the officer, he was there on behalf of the Chief Constable as part of a new enquiry into allegations that Jacobs was in possession of stolen goods. Once again, it proved to be a fruitless investigation but Jacobs was more convinced than ever that Stark and Schultz, through their membership of the watch committee, were pulling strings within the police to hound him out of office.

By now Jacobs was straining at the leash and at a council meeting in January 1944 he duly snapped and went public, recounting the Pontefract episode and his claim that the police, under Wells' instructions, had tried to pin a charge on him by offering a bribe to a third party. In short, he claimed the police were conducting a witch hunt against him. For his part, Wells was forced to deny the claim.

After the council meeting and the resulting damaging newspaper headlines, the Chief Constable attempted to draw a line under the subject by inviting Jacobs to a private meeting on the pretence of discussing the matter of force discipline. In fact, when the two men did meet Wells allegedly asked the councillor to withdraw his bribery allegations in return for the dropping of all police investigations into Jacobs' affairs. As part of the deal, an agreed statement would also be released to the press indicating that any differences between the two sides had now been resolved. A self-imposed ban on any future public pronouncements on the issue was also agreed. However, Jacobs would later claim the meeting also included a confession by Wells that he had been ordered to 'get' the troublesome councillor by Stark and Schultz. Needless to say, that disclosure didn't appear in the agreed statement.

Wells duly took the matter of the proposed press statement back to the watch committee for approval, but Jacobs wasn't happy. Not only did he feel his public image had been compromised, he also believed Wells had deliberately chosen not to read out a full explanation of the terms under which he had agreed to withdraw his original allegations. Instead, he claimed Wells had simply told the committee that he had wanted to withdraw his comments without making any reference to the other side of the deal.

The matter stubbornly refused to go away despite the best efforts of the Labour-led watch committee, and Jacobs eventually submitted a formal complaint to the Home Office to trigger yet another enquiry. The resulting investigation was headed by London magistrate Geoffrey Raphael who, in his final report, succinctly summed up the political climate in Hull in the early 1940s. 'It was Mr Wells' misfortune he took up his appointment in Hull at a time when the council, and in particular the watch committee, were divided into factions involving the bitterest hostility.'

Raphael's investigations were carried out behind closed doors and a copy of his eventual report was sent to the city council. However, it was not made public, after the Home Office refused to allow its release, claiming that, because it mainly dealt with matters involving the efficiency of the force rather than the conduct of the Chief Constable, it should be the subject of a lengthy disclosure order banning its publication. To the fury of Jacobs and his supporters, the ban was subsequently confirmed at 80 years, preventing any release until 2027.

The ban led to protests from some councillors, including one who threatened to hire a venue and read the full report in public to anyone who cared to attend. The watch committee also came under renewed pressure as some believed its less than enthusiastic pursuit of the allegations against the Chief Constable was all part of a wider cover-up. Even so, the contents of the report were shared among a select few at the council, and the wheels were put in motion to start disciplinary action against Wells, at which point he signed off sick and never returned to his job. The Chief's eventual request for early retirement on the grounds of ill-health provoked further clashes on the politically divided watch committee, which eventually begrudgingly agreed after initially refusing to grant him a medical pension.

The report was finally made in public in 1993 after renewed media interest in the case, but its contents hardly seemed to justify the early departure of a Chief Constable and the amount of political vitriol he provoked. It revealed that Raphael had examined five accusations made by Jacobs against Wells. The first involved the Chief Constable's alleged authorisation of the investigation into Jacobs' supposed possession of stolen goods; the second and third related to what Jacobs claimed had been the unauthorised private meeting between the pair after his full council outburst; the fourth charge was that Wells had deliberately misled the watch committee by editing details from their agreed joint statement; and the fifth accusation centred on a claim by Jacobs that Wells had sent officers to persuade him to refrain from taking any further action.

The report rejected all the allegations bar two, concluding that Wells had acted improperly by conducting an unauthorised meeting with the councillor and, more importantly, had grossly misrepresented the position to the watch committee. It also revealed the Chief Constable had not been averse to trying to catch out his accuser by any means possible, having had a hidden recording device installed in his office, to bug his conversations with Jacobs. The bug had been fitted in secret and paid for using public funds without any authorisation from the watch committee.

A postscript to the story was, perhaps, inevitable considering the characters involved. Not surprisingly, at the heart of it were Alfred Jacobs and his old adversary Archie Stark. It occurred in July 1948 when Sidney Lawrence, Wells' successor as Chief Constable, received a very odd telephone call informing him about a fatal accident which had happened at the city's main bus station. The accident, it transpired, was not the reason for the call. Instead, the Chief was being asked whether he would grant permission for Stark to be taken to Leeds in a police car so that he could catch a connecting service to Blackpool.

Stark had been at the station in the immediate aftermath of the fatality and had rushed to help. In doing so, he missed the bus he intended to catch to Blackpool, where he was due to join his wife for a short holiday. Concerned that she would be worried about him not being on the bus when it arrived, and with no direct telephone contact number for her in the resort, he asked a police constable at the scene whether he could be immediately driven to Leeds where the bus was scheduled to make its next stop.

Lawrence faced a dilemma. Allowing a police car to be effectively used as a taxi for an alderman going on his holidays was not exactly a proper use of public property. The new Chief Constable had only briefly met Stark once before at an official function but probably knew of his colourful background, as well as his lengthy service on the watch committee. After asking for further details on the help given by Stark at the scene of the accident, Lawrence found a sufficient reason to give his approval. He decided that as the alderman had gone out of his way to assist the police in the station, the use of the police car to ferry him to Leeds could be justified on this exceptional occasion. He also cited the potential worry his wife might have faced had Stark not been on the bus when it arrived in Blackpool.

Aware his judgement would almost certainly be questioned, Lawrence instructed both the police constable involved and the bus station inspector to submit reports detailing his conversations with them about the incident. He also started drafting a lengthy statement of his own for the watch committee.

Inevitably, the story quickly reached the ears of Councillor Alfred Jacobs who embarked on yet another pursuit of his long-standing enemy. He quickly arranged a meeting with Lawrence on the pretext of wanting to discuss another matter, only to make the most of the opportunity to inform the Chief Constable that he had been approached by several people concerned about Stark's request. Lawrence outlined the reasoning behind his authorisation but Jacobs wasn't going to let it lie. Immediately afterwards he telephoned the town clerk E H Bullock demanding an inquiry.

Jacobs' wish was granted but he did not get the result he was looking for. The inquiry by the watch committee saw Stark represented by his long-time ally Leo Schultz, much to the annoyance of the committee chairman Harold Fairbotham, who was not in favour of witnesses being represented. 'If my representative is not allowed to act on my behalf, I shall not be prepared to appear,' said Stark. He duly won his first battle but the committee's eventual report recommended his resignation from the council. Boosted by the knowledge that the Director of Public Prosecutions had decided against instigating any criminal proceedings over the matter, Stark refused to budge. Jacobs' last throw of the dice was to lobby for a vote of censure by the full council, and his Municipal Association Group duly tabled such a motion.

The resulting debate was so bad-tempered, with Jacobs and Schultz in particular hurling insults and accusations at each other, that at one point another councillor reminded everyone that a party of schoolchildren was present in the public gallery who should be allowed to leave if the two wanted to continue shouting at each other. The motion was finally defeated by just two votes and Stark kept his place on the council, while Councillor Fairbotham went to great lengths to ensure the old practice of using police cars to ferry watch committee members around the city and beyond was all over and done with. 'From now on no police cars would be used for any other purpose than police duty,' he said. 'I firmly believe Alderman Stark had been living in the past. A car came along and he felt entitled to get in and be taken on his way to try to catch a bus to Blackpool,' he said.

SOME OTHER PUBLICATIONS AVAILABLE FROM HIGHGATE PUBLICATIONS

HULL DAILY MAIL
The story of a local newspaper founded in 1885
by Barbara Robinson.
Price £7.50

A NEW LOOK AT KINGSTON UPON HULL
An illustrated guide to some of Hull's most interesting buildings
by Trevor Galvin.
Price £7.50

BACK OF BEYOND
Memories of Life on a Holderness Farm 1903-1925
by Alice M. Markham.
Price £9.95

**Available direct from Highgate Publications,
24 Wylies Road, Beverley, HU17 8AP
Telephone (01482) 866826
Postage and packing FREE
or send SAE for a complete book list**